Living with a
Learning Difference
(Disability)

THROUGH THE EYES OF THE LD CHILD

LIVING WITH A LEARNING DIFFERENCE (DISABILITY)

RICHARD A. EVANS, JR, PH.D.

outskirts
press
Denver, Colorado

The opinions expressed in this manuscript are solely the opinions of the author and do not represent the opinions or thoughts of the publisher. The author has represented and warranted full ownership and/or legal right to publish all the materials in this book.

Living with A Learning Difference (Disability)
Through the Eyes of the LD Child
All Rights Reserved.
Copyright © 2012 Richard A. Evans, Jr, Ph.D.
v2.0

Cover Photo © 2012 JupiterImages Corporation. All rights reserved - used with permission.

This book may not be reproduced, transmitted, or stored in whole or in part by any means, including graphic, electronic, or mechanical without the express written consent of the publisher except in the case of brief quotations embodied in critical articles and reviews.

Outskirts Press, Inc.
http://www.outskirtspress.com

ISBN: 978-1-4327-7924-5

Outskirts Press and the "OP" logo are trademarks belonging to Outskirts Press, Inc.

PRINTED IN THE UNITED STATES OF AMERICA

Preface

IN 1976 WHILE I was struggling in high school, special education was just finding a foothold in the hallways of America's educational systems. By the end of that year, regular and special educators were discussing such issues as roles, responsibilities, needs, and resources to fulfill the mandates of federal legislation (PL 94-142), but during that time I became just another high school dropout. I dropped out of high school never understanding why school was so difficult for me until 1992 while having a psychological evaluation for depression. I was diagnosed with two distinct learning disabilities (Developmental Reading Disorder and Expressive Writing Disorder). Later Dyslexia and Attention Deficit Hyperactivity Disorder would be added to the list. You would have thought this might only add to my depression but it did not. Quite the opposite, just knowing that my problem had a name and that I was not stupid gave me **hope**.

I now know that just because I learn differently and write poorly, it does not mean that I am stupid.

Learning in a non-traditional manner means that academically I do things a little differently. In 1992 I returned to school after getting a GED and enrolling in college. Through trial and error and long perseverance, I found that I could function in an academic setting. In 2004 I completed my academic endeavors by earning a PhD in Educational Psychology from Texas A & M University.

Currently I am an Associate Professor and Special Education Program Advisor at Angelo State University in San Angelo, Texas. My understanding of learning and reading difficulties allows me to better prepare future teachers to teach special needs students. My teaching certification and licensures include elementary education, special education, science, mathematics, and an administrator certificate. My personal goal is to share with others that there is hope for struggling students.

This book is written to be a source of **hope** for everyone that reads it, especially for individuals with learning challenges, their parents, their teachers, their family, and their friends. It exposes some of the struggles individuals with Dyslexia, Learning Disabilities, or Attention Deficit Hyperactivity Disorder (ADHD) may experience. Most of the first section of the book comes from my journal notes which I wrote as I worked through some of my problems during the first 20 years of my life. The remainder comes from my education and personal experiences of learning about and living with my learning differences. I have had the displeasure of meeting individuals who think my success is a coincidence and that I am an exception to the rule; however, I disagree. I am not an exception to the rule, I am the rule and I happily proclaim: All Students Can Learn.

Foreword
BY DR. KAREN CLEMONS

IT WAS MY privilege and pleasure to have Dr. Richard Evans as a student in both undergraduate and graduate classes at Angelo State University. While there, he became a member of Kappa Delta Pi, an honorary society for high-achieving students. I never questioned Richard's ability as a student, although I probably marked his writing errors more than was appropriate under the circumstances. As far as I know, Richard never asked his professors to give him special consideration because of his learning difficulties. Before enrolling at ASU, Richard first had to obtain a GED, and he then entered college as a student who was more than a decade older than most of his peers.

When I began teaching, I taught students of all ages in many educational settings and subjects. I became a certified Reading Specialist shortly after receiving my M.S. degree and began teaching children with reading problems full time for eight years. During that time, I took many semester hours of doctoral courses in which I continued to analyze various reading and writing disorders as well as methods recommended for helping these students succeed. However, after reading Richard's book, I now realize that he has taught me as much as I may have taught him about how to teach these students successfully.

I was not fully aware of Richard's many struggles as a student until I read this book. He truly has overcome tremendous challenges of many different kinds to become a very successful teacher, professor, and mentor to his students. He has received formal recognition from students as the professor they consider **being** most outstanding.

In this book, Richard shares knowledge and personal insight about different types of confusion that children with learning difficulties may experience in their early reading and writing experiences. He also shares from personal experience the effects of a poor self-image due to negative experiences with both teachers and peers due to learning difficulties. These harmful effects do not always end after students leave school and may persist throughout their lives.

Fortunately, this is not a "doom and gloom" book. Students' weaknesses may become their strengths, and numerous methods can help students succeed. This book is a useful resource for teachers, university students preparing to be teachers, parents, and others who want to help students overcome learning difficulties. When struggling students succeed, their opportunity improves greatly to become happy individuals who will not experience the frustrations and unhappiness that many less successful students in the past had to endure.

Table of Contents

I. Foundational Baggage
Introduction 1
At-Risk From The Very Beginning 5
Early School Difficulties 17
Secondary School Years 33

II. The Perceptions
The Way I See The World 53
Academic Issues To Consider 55
Non-Academic Issues 73
Strengths 81

III. Resilience
Nikao 89
Physical Buoyancy 97
Emotional Plasticity 109
Spiritual Character 121
Final Thoughts 127

Reference 139

I. Foundational Baggage

(Key painful memories, hurts, or negative experiences carried forward from the past that have impacted my future emotional experiences)

Introduction

THIS IS VERY hard for me to do—to sit down and try to remember the many painful and agonizing memories of school experiences and other difficult times which previously I have chosen to block from my mind. I spend hours at my computer writing about the memories I can recall, and then at night I revisit the nightmares—especially the countless miserable days I endured in school. Looking backward while writing each day leaves me exhausted; still, I feel compelled to push on. I also write because it is good therapy. It helps me to work through and to overcome present problems as well as to understand cycles and patterns that still affect my life. Most of all, however, I want to help others with learning differences not to suffer because of their prolonged negative experiences.

My learning disabilities are only part of the problem, and because of them I have developed other problems such as emotional or foundational baggage. Foundational baggage consists of painful memories, hurts, and negative experiences which, when carried forward from the past, inevitably impact future emotional experiences. Combinations of these differences create even more problems. It is like telling a lie and then having to tell other lies to correct the original. My life has been filled with a variety of primary problems.

Through the years, I tried unsuccessfully to compensate for these problems. The more adjustments I made for the primary problems, the more messed up my life became. It would have helped immensely if someone had told me that it was okay to be a little different—that just learning differently did not mean I was stupid.

Learning differently does not mean that I am altogether different from what is considered to be normal. It just means that I do some things differently. For me, it means that I work most effectively out of the right side of my brain, not the left side which is preferred by most people. It means I need to see the whole picture first and spend time experiencing the idea. It means I live in a three-dimensional space in which I experience each of these dimensions and even get lost in them sometimes. It means I want to discover the parts of the idea or object for myself even though I often need help. It means I must discover in different ways the knowledge that others learn through memorization.

I also know that learning differences are not a curse; they are a plus when students work hard, are taught what they need to learn, and are not afraid to utilize their strengths. There are many people with learning disabilities such as dyslexia and ADHD (attention deficit/hyperactivity disorder) who are very successful.

They succeed when they develop self-confidence and knowledge about who they are and how they think. When their ideas and approaches are different from the mainstream, they do not just assume they are stupid; they courageously test the possibility that it is their own creativity at work.

I want to encourage you as readers of this book to become aware of the unique strengths and weaknesses of individuals with learning differences and to help them build upon these. It is imperative for students and adults with learning challenges to understand their abilities, strengths, and weaknesses so that they can make intelligent choices about their future. I am writing this book to share my life and its many obstacles, challenges, experiences, and even disabilities. For the complete picture, we will explore three major areas which I have titled Foundational Baggage, Perceptions and Nikao.

Foundational Baggage explores the at-risk factors of my early life and the issues that impacted my academic and social development. In Perceptions I explore how I view the world—how I learn, why I think the way I do, and some of the challenges I have. Then the last part explores nikao or resiliency from two different perspectives. The first perspective is the viewpoint of a parent or teacher fostering and supporting resiliency in a struggling individual. The second focuses on how an individual such as myself (with learning difficulties) uses the components of resiliency to find success in the real world.

At-Risk From The Very Beginning

I WAS BORN in 1959, in the small Central Texas town of Brady which had a population of about 6,000. My struggles started even before I was born. My birth was difficult; I was in a breach position—feet first instead of headfirst—and the umbilical cord was wrapped around my neck. The umbilical cord had pulled me to an abnormal fetal position, causing my head to be tilted sharply to the left; a condition I now know is called Torticolis. Torticolis is a condition of continuing and uncontrollable tightening of the neck muscles causing the head to be twisted to an abnormal position. Our small town doctor was more than a little uneasy about which problem he should handle first, but God had his hand on me and into the world I came, an almost perfect baby boy.

My first few years of life were spent in the town of my birth. Around age four, my parents packed up and moved from the little town of Brady, Texas, to Fort Worth, Texas. My first real memories were those of my family living on Sylvania Avenue in Fort Worth. When

I speak of my family, I am referring to one brother, Sammy, who is two years younger than I, Loretta, a sister, who was born one year after Sammy, and at this particular time, my mother was expecting my youngest brother, Calvin.

For the most part, I believed I was a normal child. I recall how much I loved to watch machinery working. It was fascinating to sit and watch the movement of belts and tumbling gears. For as long as I can remember there was always a feeling that I could relate to things that were mechanical. There was something magical, yet systematic, about the way these contraptions worked. Any type of machinery fascinated me and I wanted so much to be a "helper," but I was always too small. I loved to watch my dad work on his pickup and especially liked my mother's wringer type washing machine.

The wringer washer sat in the middle of the back yard, and it had a long extension cord. A long drain line was also attached to it and was moved around to water the garden. A washtub sat on a stump in front of the washing machine to catch the clothes as they came out of the wringer.

With two toddlers and an infant, Mom was constantly washing diapers, and it intrigued me to watch how that wringer worked. My mother would put the wet clothes into the wringer while they were full of water, yet they almost instantly came out the other side flat and almost dry. I sat and watched, trying to think of a way to help. Sometimes she gave in and allowed me to help her place the smaller pieces of clothing into the wringer and then removes them from the other side. Next I helped her hang them on the line to dry, and later that evening we brought them into the house to fold and put away.

Once when my mother was washing clothes, the telephone rang and she headed into the house to answer the phone. I decided that this was the perfect time for me to help her. I was very excited as I retrieved one of the wet diapers out of the washing machine and attempted to run it through the wringer. While trying to put it in the wringer, I found that I was too short to reach it without someone to hold me up. I didn't give up though. I carefully climbed up the side of the machine and by stretching as far as I could, I managed to reach the wringer. As I slowly put the diaper into the wringer, it caught my hand and pulled me up the side of the washer, and the diaper and my arm both went through the wringer. I screamed for help, and my mother came running out the door to rescue me from the wringer.

By the time Mom arrived, the wringer had stalled out, and apparently I had blacked out because I do not remember anything else. Mom opened the wringer, pulled my arm out, and as she prayed, she ran and carried me to the neighbor's house. The neighbors looked me over and the prognosis was good, no broken bones—but they suggested that I should not help wash clothes for a while. The odd thing was, I still was not scared of the machine. Instead, I tried to figure out how I could prevent this mishap from happening again. In fact, the majority of my learning experiences came at the expense of a mishap. I cannot remember anything that really went right—only failures and I constantly wished I could do something right!

There were a large number of reoccurring wounds on and about my body because I constantly stumbled and fell. A few stitches here, a few there, and I would be up and running again. All of this happened to a kid who was really not very active. I just seemed to be going the wrong way at the wrong time or standing in the wrong place when someone else needed to go past me.

There were times when just getting into the car was a big deal. One such mishap was on Thanksgiving Day in November 1964. I had gone with my dad and his brothers to the shooting range to sight in a gun. While on our drive out to the range I had noticed a few pieces of what looked like candy in the back of the car. As soon as we arrived at the range and everyone exited the car, I returned to explore what was in the back. Before I could even get in the car, I landed face first into the door jam. The next thing I remember is the doctor telling me that the needle was going to hurt a little. I felt every stitch that the doctor put in my forehead that day, and I still carry a nice little scar from it.

Summertime brought its own problems. One time when I was playing in the pasture across the road from my grandparents' house, I fell face first into the prickly pear cactus. My mother, grandmother, and two of my aunts had to hold me down and pick the needles out. Then the following summer on a trip to view the construction of a dam in Brady, our whole family had walked to the top of the earthen dam. I was so excited that when we headed back to the car, my head got ahead of my body and I tumbled over and rolled all the way to the bottom of the dam. My fall did not require any stitches, but it did take a month to heal.

Shortly after that, I received a bike for my birthday. I still remember how uncoordinated I was while trying to ride that bike. I was about five years old and it was one of those big bikes with wings and long fenders. Today I remember it as a bicycle with big training wheels on the side, and the bar in the center looked like a small gas tank. I was so uncoordinated that every time I rode it, I fell flat on my face. I spent more time under the bicycle than on top of it. As I recall, I was still using the curb and the porch to help me get started on my rides long after my younger brother was riding his bike without help. As much as I liked mechanical devices, they did not seem to like me.

If being clumsy did not cause enough problems, the problem with my neck started to cause severe headaches. I found that it was a lot easier for me if I chose to do activities which would not require much movement. I played with miniature soldiers, cowboys, and Indians as well as toy trucks and tractors which required very little activity. I often chose small isolated areas where I played by myself. Some favorite places to play were behind the couch, behind and under a large recliner, and behind hedges in the front yard. These places were always balmy, dark and deserted—just the place for me. I also started to spend a lot of time daydreaming.

Poor Self-Esteem

When we moved to Fort Worth, my father got a job as a butcher with a large grocery store chain and quickly became the store manager. For the family, this meant more income and a better house, but a lot less time with my father. The new job also brought more stress for my dad and consumed much more of his free time. Dad started to drink during this time which caused problems for the whole family. Mother reared four stair-step children who were born within a five-year period, and she had to do it mainly by herself.

My mother did the best she could with only a 7th grade education. She had experienced problems in school with reading, writing, spelling, and excessive absenteeism. Never having lived in a big city, my mother's fears and anxieties became our fears and anxieties. Her worries included concerns about my dad, our neighbors, and all of the other fears that the big city can impose on a small town girl.

Nevertheless, I thought I was a perfect child living in a perfect world. I had never lived where there were other children in the neighborhood. Therefore, I was extremely excited to have other kids to play with, although they were not as excited about me. It hurt me badly that they laughed at me and did not want to play the games I did. The older kids called me "10 till 6" because my head was tilted slightly 7 to 8 degrees to my left due to my birth defect of a stiff muscle in my neck. In my own mind, I had not seen myself as different from them even though my head was a little tilted.

It was depressing. I did not understand about

cliques and how it was natural for them to pick on the new kid. I cried for days and wished that I had a friend who would accept me and play with me. I just decided since they did not like me, I would not like them either. I tended to be a loner even at school.

Eventually I did make friends with the neighborhood kids; and even though some of them still made fun of me, I managed to get along. There was always that underlying concern about why I was different, but my mother always told me, "Don't worry, you will grow out of it." I waited and waited, but it just never happened.

I never really understood why my head was tilted or why the other kids thought it was funny. I also did not understand why my head hurt all the time. There was a nagging pain in the back left side of my head, but I thought it was normal. I assumed that everyone had that pain and that I was not tough enough to handle it. I cried myself to sleep many nights because of my headaches.

I learned very quickly that when I was less active, my head did not hurt as much. Also, I learned that if I played by myself no one would laugh at me. From that point on I began to withdraw from those around me. I chose to block all painful emotions from my mind. I learned to turn off emotions such as anger, fear, sorrow, and sometimes even expressions of joy. I did not get mad, sad, or even happy when it came to relationships. I just pushed those emotions deep down inside. I developed within myself an unspoken principle: "stay away from people because people will hurt you—that is just what they do." Therefore, the majority of my childhood memories are of playing alone in some out of the way place where no one could find me.

First School Experience

I do not remember being read to as a child. Neither my mother nor my father completed high school. Eventually, my father managed to complete his high school requirements through correspondence courses; however, my mother did not. Looking back, I can see that my mother had some of the same problems that I did; she could not read or write very well. Unfortunately, her lack of education only added to and compounded my problems.

My first recollection of school was preschool in Fort Worth, an eight-week program where we spent half a day coloring, eating cookies, and drinking milk from great big half-pint cartons. It was exciting, but scary, too. The first day of school resembled a big party, and the teacher and students were all so preoccupied with the activities of the day that no one noticed that I was lost and confused. However, there were so many toy trucks and building blocks that I still thought of it as heaven.

I do not think I actually learned anything. We played a lot—running and jumping—which was fine for most of the kids; however, it caused me to have severe headaches. Around the same time, my parents bought a nice little house in Fort Worth just down the street from the school where I would start 1st grade the next year.

From the beginning of first grade, my mother,

brothers, and sister walked me to the corner where they would watch me cross the street and walk up to school. First grade was not as much fun as my preschool experience had been. There was little opportunity to play with toys as we had the year before. All the kids laughed at me and asked, "Why do you walk around with your head crooked?" I quickly decided I did not like school.

My first grade teacher read books to us, and it fascinated me how the teacher could interpret the symbols and words on those pages. This is my first memory of having been read to. I do not really remember learning any ABCs or words. However, I do remember making various mistakes when I was given directions.

I recall once when the teacher gave instructions for a little trip outside. She said, "Class, we will go outside by the library and look at what is going on for the Halloween carnival, and then we will come back, get our lunches, and go to the cafeteria." I could not think that quickly; all I heard was, "We will go to the cafeteria," and I broke out of line to run get my lunch. I had not processed everything she said, only the last part. So, guess who was standing on the fence while everyone else got to enjoy recess? I do not even remember what the carnival looked like because I was so worried about not having my lunch when we got to the cafeteria. There was a great fear building up inside of me. I felt that I was alone facing a world that I would never understand.

Along with the misunderstandings of what was being said, my headache problems continued to get worse. I was becoming less and less active, and this set into motion a deeper process of becoming withdrawn. It is no wonder that I ended up with some sort of phobia about school. Every morning I would physically feel sick. Some mornings I even lost my breakfast before school, and this was only my first year.

I began to ask myself why the other children seemed to be so much more successful than I. Why was it, they heard and understood what was being said? There was no answer in my world to make it better. At the young age of six I did not understand, and I just wanted it to go away. As my headaches worsened, my ability to stay focused on what we were doing in class began to weaken, and my difficulty in following directions became a bigger and bigger problem.

Short Attention Span

These problems were even showing up at home. I tended to get into trouble for not picking up and putting my toys away or cleaning my room. This is normal for most kids, but when my parents told me to pick up my toys, I picked up the first load and took them to my room and then could not remember what else I should do. I simply found one of my secret hiding spots and started playing again. When confronted about what I was doing and why I had not finished picking up my toys, I actually did not know.

I really wanted to make my parents happy, but I could not get one thing finished before starting something else. I can still hear the phrase that my parents used regularly (and continued to say throughout most of my life), "R.A., you never finish anything." God, I hated to hear that phrase, but even I knew it was true.

One of my favorite little hiding spots was behind the loose material on my father's recliner. I climbed behind that material inside the recliner and played in the dim light with my little toy soldiers and cars for hours. I would become so engrossed in these activities that when my mom or dad called for me, I never heard them. One time they hunted and yelled for me until they panicked. Then, by chance, they happened to see my little foot hanging out from underneath the recliner. My dad got me out and really scolded me, but I did not understand why he complained. Now that I have been a parent, I know that he was scared. I was just so involved in what I was doing that I could turn the rest of the world off. I was totally in a world of my own which I enjoyed. I felt safe and normal when I played by myself, so I did that whenever I could.

Television excited me so much that I could not sit still to watch it. I would roll around on the floor, flip up and down, and twist around under and over things. I still have to move when watching it today, but without the rolling and flipping, of course. I do not think I watched a lot of TV when I was little, but when I did, I was consumed. I had no idea what was going on around me until my mom or dad turned it off. I will discuss more about this in the second section, The Perceptions.

Early School Difficulties

I WAS ALREADY off to a rocky start in first grade. I worked very hard to make a friend or two, but then we moved away midway through the year. In December, we moved back to Brady (the town where I was born). After only a few weeks off for the Christmas break, I came back and could not remember the names of any letters that we had learned or how to write them.

Thereafter, first grade in Brady was the pits for me. I did not understand the connection between sounds and letters. I wondered, "How do they know what sound goes with which letter?" Also, I struggled when I could not get my letters to go the right direction. I could not hold a pen or pencil very well—especially the way the teacher wanted me to. I was also confused about which hand to write with. I thought my right hand was dominant, but neither hand really felt natural. I was completely convinced there was something wrong with me. There had to be; no one else was having this problem. The other students could sing and say the ABCs and count. They also read about a boy named Tip and his dog, Mitten.

While I attempted to read the Tip and Mitten books, I could never remember what Tip and Mitten were doing. Without the pictures, I could not remember anything at all. I read that same book all semester. I can still remember that this teacher never lost her temper with me the way future teachers did while demanding, "Where are you getting those words?" She would simply say, "Richard, I don't think that's what it says. Look at it again. Now, what is that first word? Someone help him out."

She would come stand over me and point at each word and ask, "Now, what is this word and what is that word?" until I would say each word in the sentence with help from my classmates. Then she would ask me to read the full sentence for her. Even then, I still did not have the foggiest idea what that sentence said. I hated trying to read aloud; it made me feel so very different.

I was in the slowest and lowest reading group in the class. I always hoped that someone would be slower and less talented, but sadly I was always the worst. When it came my time to read I would become so nervous that I could not remember the words even when I had once known them. I tried to read the story by looking at the pictures, but it always came out wrong. Consequently, I sounded like an idiot, and no one wanted to sit by me or be my friend. No one wanted to be around the dumbest kid in class. Not Even Me!

I think some of my first grade problems were caused by differences in instruction. In Fort Worth, it was a phonics-based program. In Brady there was a "see and say" reading program. In the "see and say" program, Brady first graders were already reading three- and four-word sentences from the Tip and Mitten book. What made it worse for me is that I did not know they had already been doing this for half of the year. In my mind, these kids could just pick up a book and start reading.

My teacher, Mrs. Simpson, was very understanding, always very nice, and tried very hard to help me. I really believe that she understood my situation and knew that I lacked exposure to the things the other students knew. But as the months went by, I still did not improve. I wondered how the other kids knew what words to say and why I could not do the same.

Reading was not my only challenge. I remember trying to draw/write the letters of the alphabet, but I just could not do it correctly. I kept writing "g" and "j" backwards. I could not remember which direction the tail curved—I wanted to curve it backwards. When writing a "b" or a "d," I could never remember which way to form the letters or even where to start writing the letter, whether at the top or bottom of the line or on the curve. I remember erasing until I would tear the page on my Big Chief tablet with my No 1 pencil, and I would have to tear it out and start over. Even recognizing a single letter of the alphabet and saying its name was difficult for me.

However, I did remember some of the numbers. When learning to count, I imagined picking up rocks. My younger brother and I would go to the barn and make small rock piles. We would then throw the rocks at the barn or go to the tank and throw them into the water. We eventually devised a game called Rock Wars. We counted the rocks and put them in piles of five or ten. The numbers stayed in my memory because of the rock piles. Unfortunately, I had no gimmick for the letters of the alphabet or the words in the book. Perhaps until first grade I had never even heard of the alphabet.

In addition to my previous problems in recognizing, remembering, and writing letters, the teacher began asking which letters made which sounds. Unfortunately, I could not associate letters with sounds, such as the letter T with the sound (t). When asked, "I would say T, I guess." After hearing the teacher's question, I wondered to myself, "How should I know?" There seemed to be no relevance in stringing sounds together to make words. When the Tip and Mitten books contained pictures, I could look at the pictures and see what they were doing, but sounding out words or recognizing whole words confused me totally. It was just more than I could grasp.

I remember singing the ABC song, but I could not understand it. I especially could not figure out the word "Lmnop" (L M N O P). We would sing A, B, C, D, E, F, G, H, I, J, K, Lmnop. I learned to sing the song, but it did not create a mental picture, and I could not relate it to the letters when I saw them. There were a few times that the teacher would call on me and ask what letter comes after K, and after much hesitation, I would finally respond "Lmnop," and everyone would laugh except the teacher. I did not really know what I had done wrong. Still today, I struggle with the order of letters in the alphabet, and I occasionally fall back on my memory of that elementary ABC song.

Sadly, at that time, my teachers probably did not have large cards with memorable illustrations such as teachers commonly have today. Individual letters are now introduced at the beginning of a word (e.g., "p" as heard in "policeman") and are accompanied by a picture (e.g., a policeman) in order to emphasize the first letter and first sound in the word. The letter is large and highlighted with color, and its sound is introduced using this memorable context. That may have helped me understand the connection between a letter and its sound more easily.

While looking after two younger brothers and a sister, my mother had very little time to help me with schoolwork. I was six years old, and I was expected to help take care of my three younger siblings who ranged in ages from four to two years of age. There was not a lot of time to spend with me on the ABCs. Although she tried, either she or I would get frustrated, and then we would stop. Over time, the tension over my reading and spelling problems began to grow.

Looking back, developmentally I think I was not ready for first grade. I probably should have been retained, which would have allowed me to complete first grade all at one school. I could not write or draw my letters by the end of first grade, and there were very few words that I could read or recall. The only thing I could do was look at the picture and guess what was happening. Surprisingly, I was fairly accurate at guessing.

Needless to say, when the school year ended, I had fallen far behind the rest of the class. Neither Mother nor Dad wanted me to be held back, so I was promoted to the second grade against the suggestion of my teacher. And being behind academically was not my only problem. After moving to Brady, I had to start making friends all over again. Unfortunately, that meant I had to work through all the laughing, name calling, and strange looks because of my tilted head.

I was extremely quiet and shy—definitely not very outgoing. I am sure part of that had to do with my nature, but part of it came out of fear. After failed attempts to fit in, I decided I would not try anymore and decided just to be a loner. This became a very useful tool in my day-to-day survival, and a pattern that I would continue to use throughout my school years.

Second Grade

The beginning of second grade was not as bad. We did finger painting and made little flower boxes with our hands. I could understand these things because I could see them. However, I was still struggling with oral directions. When listening to directions, it took me too long to process each part of what I'd heard, so by the time I heard the last part, I had forgotten what to do first. I recall one time when my mom gave me money to buy a lunch ticket for the month and to buy milk (which we had every day after recess) for just a week. I misunderstood and bought a one-week lunch ticket and bought milk for the rest of the month. The teacher had to call my mom to ask her what the extra money was for, and she could not understand why I had bought milk for a month.

I spent a lot of my free time, as well as class time, daydreaming about how to build go-carts and bicycles or how to make them work better. I would daydream about how to make my bicycle go faster and jump higher, or how to build a secret clubhouse. I tore up many a good bicycle trying to build something bigger, better, stronger, longer, and faster. The crazy thing was that although I wasted a lot of time daydreaming about improving the design of the bike, I still could hardly manage to ride it the way it was.

I do not remember a great deal of my childhood in Brady except we lived in the country, and the only kids I had to play with were my younger brothers and sister. We played little games that we made up as we went along, but mostly we just played imaginary games. I could spend hours just playing by myself, and it did not seem to bother me much. However, as I got older I began to miss not having many friends to play with, so I just decided to have a few make-believe friends of my own. Most young kids do this, but I kept mine longer than usual.

Through my second grade year, there seemed to be four or five of us who were considered the "dumb kids." I am not sure the teachers said this, but we thought we were, and that is what mattered. This became normal for us, and it seemed that the teachers did not expect a lot from us. I continued to fall farther and farther behind until the third grade.

It was during my third grade year that my original

first grade teacher who was now working with children with reading problems suggested that I might be dyslexic. She made the suggestion to my parents that I should have special reading help or perhaps be tested. My parents were not very receptive to the idea that their child was less than perfect. I don't remember exactly what they said, but to me it sounded something like "There's no way my son is retarded."

Third Grade

Third grade was the year I began to think I was different even more than I had before. My regular third grade teacher expressed concern over the problems I was having with reading and spelling. She thought I was having trouble with my eyesight and my hearing, so they planned to have this checked. In addition, the teacher and my parents thought that if I had some extra help with reading and spelling, I might be able to keep up and not have to repeat the third grade. My teacher also suggested that if I would spend less time daydreaming and more time "on task," I might be able to keep up. This was not something I was interested in doing. It was during my daydreaming adventures that I was the most normal. In my daydreams, I was successful. I did whatever I wanted, and I read like the other children. Yes, in my daydreams, I was not dumb.

The lack of any major success in third grade led to the inevitable; I was retained. When the idea of retention or failing was previously brought up to my parents, they were not receptive. However, they found themselves without a better option, so I was held back.

However, the second time through 3rd grade was not any easier. All the material seemed new, even though I knew I had seen the same worksheets before.

Teachers sometimes label students, and at this point I think I was labeled as lazy. I will admit that there were times when I decided not to try. I remember thinking, "Why try? I will still fail anyway." Another benefit from not trying was that I would get into trouble for not working, not just for being stupid. Therefore, instead of doing what I should, I spent a lot of time daydreaming.

Mr. Pearson, our principal, arranged to have my hearing and sight tested to see if either of those was part of the problem. Both were checked several times during the first semester of my second time through third grade. When they checked out okay, the conclusion had to be that I was not applying myself. However, my main problem stemmed from feeling lost and confused during much of my time in the classroom.

I remember especially having trouble with words such as "was," "saw," "who," "where," and "were." There were even times that simple words like "the" and "man" also gave me trouble. The teacher would tell me the word, but by the time I got to the next sentence, I could not remember it, just as if it were a new and different word. Even the simple little songs we sang were more complicated for me if I had to read the words as we sang.

Understanding and following directions also continued to be a big problem. It seemed that my parents had to tell me everything 25 times. It wasn't that I just ignored them or did not pay attention; it was just that I forgot what I was doing before I finished it. Even when I wanted to pay attention, I could not.

I continued to daydream and spent a lot of my time dreaming about who I could be, what I could do, or how, maybe someday, I would be someone important. I also continued to stay by myself a lot at recess. Since most of the children knew I had been held back, they made fun of me. Moreover, since I was not very outgoing, some of them believed it was their job to beat me up daily. I hated school so much that I began to have nightmares every night and would get physically sick every morning before school.

It's kind of funny, but even now when I feel down and frustrated with myself, I can still hear my 3rd grade teacher, see the look on her face, smell the liver on her breath, and feel her face in front of mine screaming, "Richard, you need to quit daydreaming and get to work." Although I knew I needed to get busy, I had gotten so good at withdrawing into my daydreaming world that I had a hard time staying in the present.

Halfway through the second time in third grade, we moved again. This time we moved to Dallas, Texas. School was a lot harder there, and of course I quickly fell behind again. I think this new teacher thought I was slower than the other students were, and since I had just moved into the district, she did not push me very hard. However, she sent me to the principal's office several times for not doing my class work or for not doing my homework correctly.

I do not remember getting into much trouble, but I can remember taking more than one of those timed reading tests in the principal's office. A lady came in and talked to me several times about what I thought of school. Sometimes she would help me with my class work and other times we would just talk. I tried very hard to keep from being a problem, but I just could not read well enough to keep up or to understand what the rest of the class was doing.

I did notice that some of the other students had problems, also. One boy often acted out in class, and one girl was very quiet and always looked like she was busy although she received low grades. The boy was often sent to the principal's office while the girl was not. I immediately decided that I was going to act like she did, because I did not like going to the office. As long as I did not have to read aloud, I would pass myself off as "being busy." I managed to succeed with this while I was in Dallas, but a new problem came up at the end of the year. We moved to Mesquite.

We moved to a brand new subdivision, and we were one of the first families to move there. I was only one of many new students, so it was much easier for me to blend in. In addition, I had a brother in third grade, a sister in second grade, and our youngest brother was in first grade, so now all of us went to school. The classes were extremely crowded and my teacher was overwhelmed with all the new students, so I did not feel I was graded on class work very much.

Fourth and Fifth Grade

My new tactic for staying out of trouble worked okay through fourth grade. I did not seem to stand out in the crowd as much, perhaps because the teachers were new and did not notice that I was falling behind. I also made some friends who were successful students which had never happened before. My brothers and sister all made good grades, and that made it better for my image at school, also, but I always came home with the poorest grades in my family.

My fifth grade year was both a very important and a very devastating year for me. This teacher was different from the rest. She wanted to see the work you were supposed to do. Just looking busy in her class was not enough, so I had to become a bit of a "smart aleck." When she kicked me out of her class for this, I was sent to the office. Eventually the office is where I spent most of my days in the fifth grade. Almost every day I was paddled for something. The good thing about this is when I got back to class; the teacher would make me sit at the back of the room. The back of the room was where the bad kids (students who were in trouble) had to sit.

You could tell by looking at my fifth grade teacher that she had a lot of years of teaching experience. She was a dark-haired woman who only stood five feet tall. Every morning at 8:00 o'clock, she took up homework and if you did not have yours, you were sent to the office for three swats (a paddling). Lord knows, I was a regular; she would look at me and I would head for the door because I already knew I was going to the principal's office. I still could not understand directions for what we were doing, so I could barely do my homework, and even when I did, I lost it before I got to school.

I could add and subtract fairly well, so I managed to do my math work in class. English and spelling always gave me the hardest times. I could not write a simple sentence using my spelling words, let alone diagram or find adjectives in my English homework. I could not write well enough in the fifth grade even to write a simple paragraph, and my handwriting was unreadable. It was at this point in my life that I knew that I had to accept the fact that I was never going to be as smart as the other kids were. I also knew that I had another seven years of schooling, and I needed to do something different in order to survive.

It also did not take long to decide that I did not want to spend all my class time in the office; my bottom just could not take it. Besides, the last few times I had gone to the office, my teacher had personally gone with me to give the swats, and she swung the paddle a lot harder than the principal had. She swung that paddle as if she gained some kind of personal satisfaction through it. I cried so hard that I could not even speak the rest of the day—of course, I only cried on the inside. I could not let any of my classmates know that I was a crybaby as well as stupid. After the third or fourth time we made the trip, I began to sense that she felt something else would be necessary to get me to do my homework. I was not very interested in finding out what that would be.

Life at home was not any better than school because I was always being grounded for being in trouble at school. My problems at school were not my parents' biggest problems, though. That was small compared to my parent's marital problems (my dad now lived somewhere else). Therefore, my problem was the safest one for them to try to handle.

Dad's drinking had gotten out of hand and it went downhill when mom tried to get him to stop. My mother had to get a job, something she had never done before. I think my siblings and I were among the first latch-key kids, long before anyone had ever heard this terminology. We stayed home and pretty much did our own thing. We watched TV, ate, messed up the house, and fought with each other.

Fortunately, in class, I managed to get a little help from some of my classmates. I met most of my friends in the principal's office, so they were not in the top 10% of my class (although, not all of them were in the lower 10% either). They just had some kind of dysfunction. One was the class clown, one was the class bully, and the others were a lot like me, "slow."

With their help, I discovered that if someone would personally and slowly show me how to do the work, I could manage to get most of it done. This was great, because once my classmates showed or explained to me what the directions said in simple language, my work started to improve. For example, if my classmate said to circle the action word instead of circling the verb, this was a great help to me. This turned out to be a gift. If I could get someone to show me how, even once or twice, I could do it. I was still making low grades in reading and spelling, but they started to come up to C's and D's which kept me out of the principal's office.

Each year I improved on this new talent. It was like

a miracle. Once I saw it, I remembered it. I would get someone to show me how to do the work, or let me look at his or her paper to see how it was done, and then I could complete the assignment on my own. I felt that this was working great, except for the fact that looking on another person's paper in class sometimes gets a person in even more trouble. Back to the office I went, and no matter what I said to explain why, it did not make my teacher or principal happy.

I tried to explain that I needed more examples, but it was a waste of time. If I could just hear someone explain the assignment in "less than fifth grade" terms, I could understand. Sadly, I got the paddle anyway. From that day on, I decided not to tell anyone else what I was doing. I just needed to get better at "my new way of learning." I knew that I must understand with only one or two examples. Since it was an extremely difficult process for me to read and follow directions, I desperately needed a new way to learn how to do that. However, finding this new way would elude me for a number of years.

Secondary School Years

YOU WILL NEVER guess what happened at the end of the fifth grade. You guessed it, my Mom and Dad agreed to try to work out their problems, and we moved back to Brady. This time moving was good for me because the work in the Brady schools was a little easier, and the sixth grade was in junior high.

Junior High

In Brady there were three elementary schools that went through the fifth grade, and these three campuses were combined in the sixth grade. This helped me because many of these students did not know each other very well, and it seemed everyone felt out of place and I fit in better. The older children still gave me a hard time by calling me names; however, I was numb to my emotions—not that it didn't hurt, but I just refused to deal with it.

I did have an advantage in sports as I had played peewee football in Mesquite. When I came to Brady, I was ready to play football, but sixth graders couldn't play. Since no one else had even played football yet and I had, I had stories of my I could share. In addition, I had started to fill out a little, so the tilting of my neck was not as obvious as it had been in elementary school. With my acquired academic skills, I managed to stay in that "C" category successfully. I just seemed to fit in okay as a "Slow Kid."

As we developed a football team in the 7th and 8th grade, I found that being a year older than my peers was also a big help. I excelled somewhat at football, and this boosted my self-esteem. My math and science skills were good, and I brought these grades up to Bs. Some of the kids in my junior high classes had been in my class in my early years at Brady, so knowing some of them helped me fit in better. Even though I was certainly not the most popular, I could fit into their cliques when I needed to. It was during these years that I found out that once the teachers explained the material in class without my having to read it for myself; I could understand it to some extent and remember it. Most of the teachers in junior high knew students were not going to read the material, anyway, so they would go over the material aloud that would be on a test. When they did this, I could pass.

Now I have to clarify the statement, "I could pass." If the test was in a format which allowed me to choose the best answer or pick the best word from a word bank, I could definitely choose the correct answer 70 % of the time, but those "finish the sentence" questions and "fill in the blanks" sentences still stumped me. Normally, if I had to pull the answer out of the air,

I was sunk. I just could not do that. Even if I could have, I would not have been able to spell it well enough for the teacher to recognize it as the correct answer.

As I look back, I believe that the teachers in Junior High thought I was a student with a low IQ and thought I was probably doing the best I could. I do not ever remember being paddled for grades except from the coaches who gave licks for low grades. I do not remember making failing grades as often as I made C's and Ds. The fact that I was a year older and a little bigger also seemed to work to my advantage in Junior High School. I still was not all that outgoing, but I seemed to be accepted as long as I pretty much kept to myself. Overall, I don't really remember Junior High being that bad; however, this could be because there were so many other things going on in my family life that school seemed trivial in comparison.

Between sixth and eighth grade, my dad's drinking problem had grown into a major drinking problem. My mother had some problems herself while trying to deal with his problem. My dad's drinking problem was so dramatic for her that I was concerned she was headed for a nervous breakdown. My dad started his own trucking business during my eighth grade year, and this was a financial struggle for my family. This new stress accelerated my dad's drinking problem and diminished my mother's mental and emotional capabilities.

If we were not at home at the proper time, my mother would panic. If my father did not come home, she would hunt for him. This is something she had been doing for years and continued to do so. There had been times in Mesquite and Dallas when she would put all of us kids in the car and drive around to all the local bars until she found his pickup. Then she would go in, leaving us in the car while she tried to talk him into coming home.

My dad's trucking business, over the next few years, grew into several trucks (18- wheelers) and a service shop, but he drank almost all of the time. Sometimes he would be gone for days at a time and we would not know where he was. My mother tried to handle her problems, hold the family together, keep the trucks going, take care of the house, and rescue my dad when he was out drinking. My brothers and I spent most of our free time working on trucks. We worked from the time we got home from school until we were too tired to work anymore at night. Some weekends we actually worked all night after my dad's fleet had grown to 8 big rigs and trailers.

Sometimes, after a long day of working on trucks, my mother would wake me up at 1:00 or 2:00 in the morning to go with her to hunt for my dad. God, I hated doing that! We would ride around for hours, sometimes all night. Sometimes we found him, other times I would fall asleep in the seat of the car until mom stopped looking. When we found him, then one of us would go in and try to convince him to come home.

I especially hated it when I had to go in. Sometimes I prayed that we would not find him when it was my turn to go in. I knew my father would be mad at us for coming after him. He would start to put me down, and when he got loud, everyone would laugh and stare at me. That made me want to cry, but crying would have only made it worse. He would tell me to go home and leave him alone. The sad thing was that when he was sober he did not remember anything he had said. But I did.

I could not understand his behavior. Did he really think and feel that way about me? My mother told me not to listen to him when he was drinking because he didn't know what he was saying. It was at that time in my life that I decided I would build a wall between my father and me. Although I might have to hear what he said, I did not have to accept it. I really think I started to hate him, but hating him made me sad -- after all, you should not hate your parents, should you?

High School

Knowing what I know now, it was fortunate I could compete academically in high school at all. It is also a wonder that no one had yet identified my problems. The year was 1975, and the Federal Government had issued Public Law 94-142, originally known as Education of the Handicapped Act. This was the first major piece of legislation dealing with the issues of Special Education.

My freshman year began one week before regular classes started, and it started on the football field. It was to my advantage that we all wore oversized uniforms because it covered the tilt of my head better, and there was not much required reading in the freshman playbook. It seemed this could be my year. Since I had been very successful in football the year before, the varsity coaches treated me as if I were an asset.

Working on trucks all summer had really paid off. I was quick off the line and my upper body strength gave me a real advantage for the first week of practice, but once school started the advantage started to fade. The first problem was with my neck because the increased activity caused my headaches to intensify. As the headaches increased, my performance began to dwindle, and the harder I tried to shake it off the more the pain increased. I became increasingly withdrawn and reserved.

It did not take that long for the coaches to mark me as uncommitted and lazy. I could see it on their faces. They were yelling at everyone else, but when they directed their remarks at me, it seemed to be with ire and disgust. I felt that everything they said was more personal than it had been earlier. Football was not nearly as much fun in high school as it had been during my junior high years.

My freshman year also was a scary experience mainly because I still had not really learned how to fit in, and it seemed too late to change at this point in my life. Not hanging with the other students made me even more of a target for the bullies at high school. Basically I was pushed on and punched by members of every clique at school, and even nerdy band students avoided me.

I found it really important to isolate myself. Having friends required me to try to achieve and perform as they did in order to measure up to their expectations.

I could not take the chance of being compared with them; I knew I couldn't measure up. I had a problem, and my problem was feeling stupid.

I worked very hard at being almost invisible. I preferred not to be noticed by students or teachers. A benefit of being invisible is that I was never called on. I would sit at my desk with my pencil in my hand and look like I was busy. I never stood out in the class. When someone looked at me, I appeared to be working. However, I was caught more than once with a pencil in my hand and a book and paper on my desk while I was sound asleep. My teachers would sigh and say, "This is why your work is only half complete." What could I say, they were partially right in their opinion about my lack of effort, but even if I had worked all the time, I wouldn't have achieved much more.

In classes where being invisible just didn't work, I then would fling anything that could be flung across the classroom. My time was spent making paper wads, bouncing them off the walls, and starting arguments with anyone I could. You name it—I did it, but that was my way of coping. It was a mechanism I used as a last resort, but I used it effectively. Unfortunately, I discovered that there were major disadvantages for both being invisible and for being the class clown. Both of these affected my ability to develop social skills, lifelong friendships, meaningful relationships, and a personal relationship with a member of the opposite sex.

I spent most of my free time daydreaming, but I no longer dreamed about how to build stuff like go-carts and bicycles. No, I dreamed—or should I say wished for—something more out of life. I wanted to be able to read without stuttering or maybe for once to pass a spelling test. I wanted to answer a question in class where I could give the right answer. I dreamed of being able to explain and diagram a simple sentence. Really, I guess I dreamed that for once I could just feel normal.

    I actually did well in a few classes such as consumer math, athletics, agriculture, and art. There were also times when I even performed skillfully in history, science, language arts, and even reading, but those times were rare. Those successful times actually confused me the most. Whenever the teacher told the whole class how hard this assignment was going to be, the other students' grades dropped down while mine went up. I remember on one of these occasions the teacher requested that I stay after class. She told me how excited she was that I had finally decided to apply myself in her class and how she would be expecting to see these kinds of grades more often.

    For the life of me I did not know what I had done differently. I tried to read the chapter, but my reading ability was no better than before. In addition, I hate to admit it, but I took fewer notes during class than normal. Eventually I discovered that the times when I did better coincided with the times my teacher added a great amount of detail about what was happening in the chapter, and I just pretended it was a movie that I had daydreamed. It seemed as if the teacher fueled my daydreams with her lectures. Yet later on even when the next chapter was easier and the majority of the class scored As on it, I on the other hand failed because not as much detail had been given in lectures.

I think my freshman year was the first time I started developing a plan about quitting school, but there were several reasons I couldn't. First, I was not old enough, and second, my parents would have killed me. I was catching so much heat at home about not finishing things that I knew I had to stick it out. I struggled through school with mostly low average grades except in reading, spelling, and algebra in which I nearly always made failing grades.

Spelling and reading had always been a problem, but algebra was a new obstacle. I could not understand why anyone in their right mind would want to use X's and Y's in math problems. It was bad enough to use ABC's in the problems, but why not go ahead and put the right number in. Why did I have to write $5 + x = y$ or $y - x = 5$ when I could write $5 + 3 = 8$ and the problem was solved. For me the answer was simple ($x = 3$ and $y = 8$), but when I got my paper back they were all marked wrong. I struggled with that crazy math all year long. It never made any sense why so much time and energy was wasted on these problems when the simplest answer to the problem would have worked just as well. Math had always been one of my better subjects, but this year even math made me feel stupid.

What had started out to be my year ended up being just another major disappointment! I ended the year below average in all areas. However, one positive thing happened my freshman year. I was able to get my driver's license, although it was only a small pebble in my nearly empty bucket of self-esteem. Other than that, I not only hated school, I now was beginning to hate life and myself.

I was very glad when summer break came even though it had its own difficulties. I loved building and repairing all kinds of items and seemed to have a natural knack for anything mechanical. I loved to start projects but didn't like to finish them. Most of the time, I felt it was a waste of time because I had already finished them in my mind. Although my parents urged me to finish, I preferred to do things I had never tried before. I didn't need to be good at an activity to feel that I understood it. I just needed to have a visual reference for it. Once I could envision the finished project, I became disinterested in it.

Last Years of High School

My sophomore year was the time that I completely came to the realization that I did not fit in. I always knew school was a struggle, but in high school, you really begin to be recognized individually. In junior high, everyone was obnoxious, but in high school you may be ranked as first, second, and so on, such as naming ones whose grades are in the top 10 or top 25 or the ones who are best looking, most ambitious, or most popular. I felt very close to the bottom in all of these areas. There were less than 100 students in my class, and if you were at the bottom of the list you knew it.

Two things kept me involved in school during my sophomore and junior years, vocational agriculture and farm mechanics. In Mr. Siler's Ag and Farm mechanics class, there were lots of hands-on activities and very few written exams. I felt successful in his classes which were demanding yet fun. He told us what we needed to understand in order to pass. In his class, we learned about electrical wiring, gas engines, working with simple circuits, AC-DC currents, and simple machines—the kinds of things that really interested me at that time. That Ag class was always a safe haven no matter how bad the day had been, and I felt like I could make it through the day if I could get to Ag. It was so nice to have one class where you were judged on what you could do with your hands versus what you could memorize for some fill-in-the-blank test.

Since as far back as I can remember, I have had an enormous appetite for understanding and experimenting with mechanical and electrical devices. I had no formal training, but radios, fans, toasters, and welded items were all part of my miniature workshop. I would find discarded things, put them in my corner of the shop, and tinker with them in my spare time. Anything that could be hooked up and made to do some kind of work interested me to find out how they worked. From gasoline engines to power saws, all of this intrigued me. I spent most of my spare time in the summer repairing small tools and appliances for people. I would make repairs for them, and they would respond by giving me a few dollars.

Football should have gone better my sophomore year but instead I struggled. I was a tight end with the responsibility of blocking and shuttling plays to the quarterback. On the field, my disability was almost invisible, but I had a coach that year who thought that he could realign my neck by increasing tension on the opposite side of the tilt of my head. I spent extra time each day in the weight room working to build up the muscles in the right side of my neck.

Torticollis was not that well known at the time, and the only major problem it caused me at that time was headaches. As my workouts increased, so did the headaches. Having my neck pulled to the right did make my neck look better, but it caused my skull to be pushed down on my spinal column. That caused my arms to ache all of the time. My head hurt so bad I could not see, but my arms felt like something was eating at the bones. They hurt all the way down to my hands.

After football season was over I went to our family doctor, and he told me I had a pinched nerve in my neck. I could not imagine how a spot in my neck could make my arms hurt, but his advice was traction. I hung this funny contraption on the door frame and put fifteen pounds of sand in it. Thirty minutes a day I would hang myself from the doorway of my bedroom.

The coach could not figure out why none of his exercises had produced the results he expected, and instead of accepting the fact that something was wrong with the procedure, he assumed that the problem was me. It was this kind of madness that made football less desirable in my eyes. It grew to the point that there was not enough reward to compensate for the agony I felt, so football was on its way out of my life.

Sophomore English was a different kind of English class than ones I had taken before. This was my first English class in which no spelling tests were given or spelling on written papers was not graded. This class was composed of a number of low performing students and was a benefit or me. We read any type of material we wanted and only had to write a simple one-page synopsis or article review. I chose to read Hotrod, Car and Driver, and Street Rodder magazines because those are what interested me at the time.

My sophomore year was the year I acquired my first car. It was a 1954 Chevy and my few friends called it "the bomb." I thought I was king of the road while everyone else thought it was a joke. However, since I was one of the first in my class to get a car, I experienced a little popularity. My dad had bought the car in near mint condition from a local businessman in town, but the first thing I did was convert it into a "poor boy street rod." I had advanced from fixing bicycles and radios to working on my own car. It was painted jet black and the back of the car was raised to allow a set of wide tires that filled the fender wells. It had a 6-cylinder motor, a 3-speed transmission, and an 8-track player under the dash that I adapted by converting the six-volt electrical system into a twelve-volt system. I only drove the car 1½ years, but in that period, it changed colors three times.

I really loved working on that car. I remember I changed the factory cloth seat covers to leopard skin spotted bucket seats which I got from the local wrecking yard. The gearshift changed from the steering column to the floor and for the last few months I drove it, most of the grill and front sheet metal were removed so I could jump it up and down a local off-road motorcycle track. I managed to survive school until the school year ended, but I was starting more and more to dream of a way to disengage from the school system. I was dreaming less and less of how to succeed in school, and increasingly about how to get out of school.

My junior year I started with even less enthusiasm than ever before. I hated school and all I could think about was getting out. I even hated football. The practices were tiring and unrewarding, and three weeks into the program I dropped out. At first I felt bad that I had dropped out, but later I began to embrace the process of quitting.

Quit-u-a-tion

During my junior year, fearing I would not be able to do the work and facing the inevitable trouble that would bring, I decided to drop out of high school. I had come to the point where I hated to go to school. Each day I was progressively sicker, and vomiting became a regular part of my daily routine. I reacted to this by avoiding school whenever I could, and I began looking for a job that didn't require much reading or writing.

It did not take much thought to decide to quit school because of the hard time I had keeping up, as well as how much I hated living at home. My dad's drinking problem had gotten much worse, and when he drank, he was hateful. Mother was not that much better. The many years of trying to rescue my dad from the bottle had left her struggling to keep her wits about her. So I got a job at a local manufacturing plant working nights, and six months later, I married my high school sweetheart.

Sadly, I dropped out of high school never understanding why school was so difficult for me. Many years later in 1992 while having a psychological evaluation for depression, I was diagnosed with two distinct learning disabilities (Developmental Reading Disorder and Expressive Writing Disorder). You would have thought this might add to my depression but it didn't. Quite the opposite, the fact that my problem had a name which meant I wasn't stupid and that gave me hope. Later I was also diagnosed as having Dyslexia and Attention Deficit/Hyperactive Disorder (ADHD).

After dropping out of high school, for seven or eight years I had many ups and downs. Multiple jobs, financial struggles, and extreme emotional outbursts (mostly in anger) caused my life continuously to spiral out of control. I not only had problems with drugs and alcohol but financially I went broke several times. Arlene's and my marriage was extremely strained, and I had two sons who began to have some of the same kind of unproductive life experiences and unhealthy home environment with which I had struggled. I was functionally illiterate (not able to neither read a newspaper nor complete a job application), and I desperately wanted all of my problems to stop.

In late Spring of 1984, my life reached a turning

point. I tell people, this was when I had a major "Come-to-Jesus" meeting. It was one of those life-changing experiences that people refer to as bottoming out. I came to a point where I had nowhere else to go; I had even taken a drug overdose hoping to commit suicide.

After 1984, it took another eight years for me before I entered college and passed my first college class. A lot of things happened in those 16 years after dropping out of high school until going to college. However, that is a totally different book. The manuscript to that book is being prepared for release and is titled *"Becoming More Alive."* So why do I tell you all of this about my early life? It is because I want you to understand some of the fundamental problems I had, the emotional baggage which kept me from digging out of this dilemma.

The majority of this first section comes from raw journal notes written in the months after my 1984 experience. My memories of the way I thought and the way I felt may not be 100% accurate, at least according to my mom, dad, brothers, or sister. They remember it a little differently, but generally we all agree on the content. Despite all these unfortunate issues, I still managed to survive.

Every child, no matter what his or her circumstance or situation is, has the potential to become more than the sum of his or her parts. No matter the past, no matter how tough the situation, children can become what they want to be when they understand their unique gifts and talents and then build upon them.

I currently have a great relationship with my wife, dad, mom, and siblings. My dad and I work together in ministry projects, and my dad now pastors a church in my hometown. My wife and I have been married over 30 years. I have two sons of whom I am very proud and four grandchildren in which I delight. I am a successful associate professor in one of the best universities in Texas, and I spend a lot of my free time doing volunteer work, speaking, and teaching both in the U.S. and Mexico.

I'm telling you my life story to let you know that even though my life started out tough, it is now turning out well. It's not because I forgot the problems of the past or that they were somehow wiped away. It's not because I no longer have learning issues (those are still evident), but it's because I eventually learned and focused on my gifts and strengths. I have built a future around my passion and my calling in life beyond past challenges to find the purpose they served in my life.

The next sections of the book give me an opportunity to share with you the way I see the world and how I now successfully process information. I will also share some of the obstacles I overcame and offer hope to those who presently need it. This information can also help teachers and parents to see students with learning differences as normal people who have challenges which can be overcome as well as enable them to help their students or children find their own pathway to success.

II. The Perceptions

Capacity to separate from the environment and other individuals to evaluate experiences of the self and explore individual unique problems and issues

The Way I See The World

IN ADDITION TO all of the early at-risk factors mentioned in the previous section, I also had some of the more common characteristics of a child who experiences difficulty in an academic setting. I was awkward, overly clumsy, and had a short attention span. My low self-esteem and other difficulties became more visible as the school years continued. Other problems I had included handwriting with occasional reversals or inversion of letters or numbers (e.g., b/d, p/g, 25/52) and sometimes in word retrieval. In addition, I had extensive problems understanding and following oral multi-step directions which were further compounded with difficulty in expressing my thoughts orally—especially when expected to respond on demand. Basically I needed longer periods of time for mental processing than the average student.

"Learning difficulty" is often the first descriptive term used when a child begins to have issues in academics, and there are many types of learning difficulties. A learning difficulty may be characterized as mild or severe, based on the level of a student's academic achievement. This difficulty may be caused by internal or external factors, and it may or may not correlate closely to the person's potential. Learning difficulties, whether they represent a learning disability or not, should always be addressed quickly before these difficulties start a negative chain reaction which often includes broad educational, social, emotional, personal, and family issues.

It is only possible to overcome learning difficulties when you understand the characteristics of the problem. Let's start by looking at how I saw the world (and still do): I don't see maps, I see models. I don't spell words, I draw them. I don't want to take risks, and I don't like surprises. I process information much more slowly than my peers, and I am primarily a visual learner. I need to see the whole picture before I can find the parts. For example if you put my belongings away where I can't see them, then I won't be able to find them. Oh, yeah, reading is the hardest thing I have ever done. So what does all this mean? Let's explore these one at a time, and I will try to let you see through my eyes the world that challenges me and other individuals with similar learning differences.

Academic Issues To Consider

THERE IS A wide range of learning problems, and the characteristics of individual students differ greatly. It is crucially important to help any child who has a problem, and as parents, friends, or individuals with leaning issues, we must become aware of how these issues should be perceived. Please consider my perceptions to be a starting point for understanding issues which children with learning differences may face each day.

Adults often have no understanding of the fear, panic, or even desperation that these children experience daily. Fear robs individuals of a future by labeling them but not getting them the help they need. The truth is that I also experienced fear and depression. Once I began to understand my learning issues and discovered how I could think and learn successfully, my fear and panic started to fade. I still struggle with desperation from time to time, but it is no longer overwhelms me. I have learned that although I think differently, I can succeed because I understand the issues.

It is my hope that by sharing with you how I learn and

■ 55

perceive the world you will be able to understand better the learning issues that you or your student, friend, or family member experiences. I hope this information will help to remove systemic barriers in order for everyone to participate successfully in education and in life and that it also provides individuals with a solid foundation for developing personal skills and strategies for success. In addition, I hope this information will encourage personal growth in seeking support in day-to-day connections with struggling individuals.

Learning differences are problems that affect the brain's ability to receive, process, analyze, or store information, but they don't prevent an individual from learning. These problems can make it difficult for a student to learn as quickly as someone who isn't affected, but once a person understands how his or her brain processes information, it can be used to good advantage. The next sections look at my academic and non-academic issues, plus I will share some of my known strengths.

Visual Learner

The first consideration is that I am a visual learner. You might ask what a visual learner is. The fact is, individuals prefer learning in particular ways, such as seeing, hearing, and experiencing things. But for the most part, there are particular methods or styles of learning which stand out. For each individual, there is a preferred learning style. Learning styles are various approaches or ways of learning. Learning styles involve educational methods particular to an individual

ACADEMIC ISSUES TO CONSIDER • 57

and are presumed to allow that individual to learn best. Most people prefer an identifiable method of interacting with, taking in, and processing stimuli or information. There are three preferred learning styles; they are visual, auditory, and tactile learning.

As a visual learner I learn by seeing things. I remember faces but have extreme difficulty with names. I can see a person and 20 years later remember their face and can recall where I knew them but I can't remember their name. I know this happens to everyone at some time or another, but for me it happens all the time. I learn through seeing, therefore a face represents a picture that I can observe and create a memorable image. Names on the other hand have no natural visual image and are difficult to retrieve.

My eyes are constantly scanning everything. I want and need to see things because I appreciate visual stimulation. I need to see maps, pictures, diagrams, color, the teacher's body, and language/facial expression to fully comprehend. In order to remember things I often have to close my eyes to visualize what it is I am trying to remember. I always think in pictures and learn best from visual displays such as diagrams and illustrations. I daydream about the subject instead of taking detailed notes to absorb the information. When I do take notes, they are doodles, pictures, boxes with information that has specific meaning to me. Most often, however, they make no sense to anyone else.

As a visual learner I look up and down and left to right to look for additional visible information. When I really connect to information I need to retain, I create "movies in my mind" of information that I am hearing, reading, or experiencing. These movies are often vivid and detailed and easily remembered. Usually, I learn best when I can see the teacher, the overhead transparencies or PowerPoint presentations, a video, and handouts. I prefer sitting at the front of the classroom to avoid visual distractions created by other students in front of me. I benefit from visually colorful presentations and illustrations which are attached to written or spoken language that is rich in imagery. To improve my learning I also make outlines of everything. I create a map of events in history or draw scientific processes and pictures to relate to many science topics.

I love to imagine in visual pictures what I will physically try to accomplish. For example, if I plan to go outside to mow the yard, I visualize the yard before I get out there and think about whether I will mow it vertically or horizontally. As I mow, I visualize other things I need to do. You may think this is not necessarily unusual; however it can be depending on its degree of importance for an individual who needs to do it in order to function well.

I tend to learn to do things by repetition, as does nearly everyone else when doing things which become automatic. When you drive to work, you probably go the same way, and when you arrive, you may not remember whether you stopped at the last stop sign. By going the same way, you don't have to think actively about what you are doing. My actions are somewhat different, though, in that I do everything visually through pictures while running on automatic. So if I

ACADEMIC ISSUES TO CONSIDER • 59

have imagined mowing the yard before I get out there, when I get outside and see that the water hose is out, instead of mowing the yard, I may do whatever I now see instead.

My secondary mode of learning is tactile and kinesthetic. Tactile learning involves physically feeling and touching an object. Kinesthetic learning pertains to movement. I process and learn by duplicating what I have seen or imagined in my mind. If I am trying to think about something but can't access it immediately, or when my mind starts processing very quickly, I have to get up and move. It is almost impossible to sit still. Even now while my wife is typing this, I am walking about the room doing multiple things. Later I may stop moving about and do the typing myself, but right now, I must move in order for my mind to process what I want to be written. This need for movement may help explain some of my moving and flipping while watching TV as a child.

Phonological Processes

I have a real problem with phonology. Phonological Processing is the proper terminology used in describing development in sound recognition. All children go through a normal process of sound and speech development in which they make appropriate mistakes. Through listening to adults speak and testing their own sound systems, children acquire information needed to identify and produce intelligible speech sounds. Phonology is, broadly speaking, the sub-discipline of linguistics concerned with the sounds of language. It is the systematic use of sound to encode meaning in any spoken human language, or the field of linguistics which studies this use. In more narrow terms, phonology (the hearing of sounds) is concerned with the use of sounds to verbalize words. Just as a language has grammar and vocabulary, it also has a sound system (phonology).

The process by which an individual hears the sounds in words is called Phonemic Awareness (PA). I don't consistently hear the individual sounds in words. PA is a sub component of Phonological Processing and is the ability to hear, identify, and manipulate individual sounds (phonemes) in spoken words. Normally for individuals to learn to read print, they must become aware of how the sounds in words work. They must understand that words are made up of speech sounds, or *phonemes*. I should note at this point, well-established research findings on reading suggest the most important skill for beginning readers is phonemic awareness. Without the ability to hear the individual sounds in words, a student will always have difficulty reading.

It is not a hearing problem (my hearing has been tested numerous times) or a phonics problem (matching the sound to the letter), it is a processing problem. I can't separate the sounds in my head. For example, you might say *"You know"* but I may hear /juno/, or you might say *"air"* but what I hear you say is /hear/. Another example might be *"I am tired,"* but I hear /I mired/. It is very challenging for me to keep words from running together, so I miss the short pauses and do not always hear the extra sounds in the word.

Reading is Labored and Slow

You can imagine how trying to understand spoken words of the English language can be impaired when a person does not hear the actual sounds of the words. The listener attempts to interpret the meaning of strange words for which he has no point of reference.

When I heard, *Do you know where the car is?* I tried to understand what each of the words sounded like. Next I would visualize what each word looked like. What does /juno/ look like? Even if I did understood and recognize the word *car,* I may not have known what *the* or *is* looked like. This was my early experience with reading. I couldn't understand the sounds and what was required to interpret the meaning of text, and it was exhausting. In about 3rd grade I discovered the concept of sight words. They had always been there, but that is when I grasped the idea. Around 6th or 7th grade I began to understand there is a subject phrase and a predicate phrase. Finally I began to understand and build a simple understanding for reading. All of my fundamental reading skills were sight based, and until then I had memorized what someone else said whether they said it correctly or incorrectly. This inability to hear sounds of individual words and to understand words and phrases clearly seriously impacted my concept and ability to spell.

Draw Words Rather Than Spell Them

Since I can't hear the sounds in words, it is difficult for me to decode words (read) or encode words (write/spell), so reading and spelling have been lifelong problems. I had no idea what the problem was until my later years, and even then it initially was by accident that I identified the issue. In order to adjust to the problem, I relied on my visual learning skills and began to memorize the visual structure of the words. The interesting thing is that the majority of the words I memorized/read came from printed materials such as dictionaries, so when I drew a word it had to be in print, not cursive. I have learned to write in cursive, but the pace in which I write is much slower than when I print. In addition, my cursive writing will have a mixture of print and cursive letters and a blend of upper and lower case letters.

Currently, the vast majority of my vocabulary was learned by sight. Much like the average reader knows that some words in our English language cannot be decoded (sounded out) easily (e.g., "the"), these words are called sight words. Sight words are words that a reader recognizes without having to sound them out. Some sight words have letter-sound relationships that are uncommon or may not follow phonetic spelling rules, and as a result are frequently learned through memorization. Some examples of sight words are *you, are,* and *said.* This is not the most effective way to learn words, but it has been the foundation for my limited literacy skills.

Sight words are the foundation for the whole-word approach (or See & Say method) in reading education. It is possible that the sight word and the whole-word approach to reading is a noteworthy teaching technique considering that 65% of adults identify themselves as visual learners. However, the majority of recent educational research suggests that phonetic based (phonics) learning strategies are more effective for languages written with alphabets, such as English. In learning to read via sight words, I started to understand that a word often represents a thing.

Top-Down Learner

Reading and spelling by sight is not all that unusual for a big-picture thinker or a top-down learner. Top-down learning involves looking at information as a whole instead of all the elements. For example, as a top down learner, I look at language as a whole and concentrate on the meaning of the passage (not just the words). As a top-down learner I need to see the whole task first and then find the parts. In other words I need to see the forest before I can see or understand what a tree is.

Not only am I a top-down learner, but also I am a right-brained person. Dyslexics are typically right brained and sometimes left-handed. As a right brained learner I am most successful when I start at (what we'd typically consider to be) the end (top) and move toward the beginning (bottom). When I see the relevance of what I am learning and understand that words communicate meaning, I am able to create the mental image. Visuals and body movement also help me make connections which are vital to understanding and remembering what the words mean. For example I don't (won't) watch a movie when I have not previewed the promotional trailer or read a review about it. The reason is that my mind will be so busy trying to figure out what is going on that I can't enjoy the visual elements or figure out what the movie is about. If, on the other hand, I have some idea where the movie is going I am able to focus my attention on the plot of the movie.

See Models Instead of Maps

I don't see maps; I see models. Why because I live in a 3-dimensional world. When in a conversation and someone tells me about an item or a place, my mind constructs a 3-D image of the item. For example if I ask a person for directions to a local shopping center, as the person begins to give the directions I begin to visualize what the path looks like. This has made life much easier, especially when I have taken time previously to drive around the community to get an overview of the area. As you may remember, I have to get the big picture, so I need to drive through and around the community and identify some landmarks. Then when I get the directions I connect them to what I have already identified. Yes, it would be easier if I could just follow the directions based on the names of roads and streets. However, because I don't decode (read) words easily, I prefer getting an overview.

I see all images as if they are real, and I perceive these images from many different perspectives. This talent works very well in the three dimensional world but leads to confusion and challenges in the two dimensional world of symbols and print. The symbols used in reading and writing, such as the letters of the alphabet, punctuation marks, and numerals, have to be seen from only one perspective for accurate recognition. Especially difficult are letters which change to another letter when seen from a different perspective in my mind. I have no problem when I picture "p" from the front in my mind, but if I see it from behind it looks like this "q." Or the letter "b" ends up a "d" from a different perspective in my mind, so to keep things straight I use key words to help keep the letters correct. Two words I use when trying to decide if the letter I am looking at or needing to write is a B, D, P or Q is "bed" and "quip."

Delayed Processing Speed

All this excessive work in understanding and remembering letters contributes to my slow processing speed (in other words, when having to think about letters, I think slower), and it delays my responses. These delays make me look and sound as if I am not very smart; however, processing speed is not the same as intelligence. In fact, it is possible to be very bright, yet process information slowly. Delayed Processing Speed refers to how quickly an individual can react to incoming information, understand it, and think about the information, formulate a response, and execute that response. Processing Speed can trigger problems that may be identified as attention, memory, organization, language, or executive functioning problems. Slow processing makes it difficult for me to shift and divide attention to different tasks, to retrieve memories, and to do tasks which require additional thinking such as problem-solving.

Slower processing speed increases my workload in basic reasoning, and it also makes it harder to recognize simple visual patterns during visual scanning tasks. I also need more time to process and understand an oral presentation of material and to complete tasks which require basic decision making. When time is a factor, this increased workload makes basic arithmetic calculations or manipulating numbers to perform reasoning tasks even more difficult. It also affects my reading for comprehension, copying words or sentences correctly, and formulating and writing passages.

Slow processing can easily be misidentified as a behavior problem, or a specific cognitive problem. In my case, slow processing interacts with other areas of functioning to create additional problems with learning. It also creates stressful situations which bring on agitation that can be misidentified as behavior issues. It is important to recognize in each individual the role-played by slow processing and to implement intervention and support strategies specifically designed to address the slow processing exhibited in each individual.

It should be noted that individuals who process information slowly and work slowly need additional time to complete tasks. They should be encouraged to create a habit of starting assignments and projects early so that they will not have to rush to complete the task. They may need to request additional time in which to complete timed tasks. Rushing will only increase errors.

Attention Issues

Focusing on whatever I am expected to do is exceedingly hard for me. As a student in class, I ended up daydreaming or sleeping, even when I really enjoyed the class. The problem extended into homework as well. I rarely finished homework because I failed to stay focused. I also had trouble doing repetitive tasks, even really simple ones. I could do them correctly; I just couldn't stay focused. Even now when I put on noise-canceling headphones or use special software to blank out everything on my screen, my mind still wanders. I'll end up doing something else, which evolves into yet another activity, and that continues endlessly until I go to bed without finishing.

Studying and paying attention in lectures also challenged me. Even now I have real trouble with directions, whether written or verbal. They confuse me greatly, and I need more than a few seconds to review them in my head to make sense of them. Even then I may need to have them repeated more than once. While thinking about them, I can't stay still. So many thoughts are racing through my head that I need to move around to release tension in order to concentrate on them better. Yet other times I find myself zoned out, thinking about something completely irrelevant instead of what I need to.

Time management is another real challenge for me. This not only applies to work; it is the same with everything—writing this book, for example. I have worked on it for 10 years, and right now I want to do something in the backyard instead. I tell myself that I should finish the book, but I continue to procrastinate, so perhaps a lack of commitment is also part of the problem. Even though I'm totally motivated and fully aware of the things I need to do in order to better myself, I usually do not stick with them long before going off track. However, eventually given enough time, I return to those activities to finish them out but it is in my time frame, not someone else's. I also tend to do a much better job in my time frame than if I'm forced to complete something before I have fully thought it through.

Authentic Learning Experiences

I really struggle with artificial learning experiences. The truth is I don't want to do things which do not matter. I like learning experiences with real-world relevance (authentic). Authentic learning experiences are those which best enable me to be engaged with the learning process. When I am able to make the learning situation meaningful and connect it to my real life events, I am better able to construct knowledge and to make learning applicable. For example, I would prefer to measure the floor in my office, calculate the number of tiles needed to redo the flooring, buy the tile, and do the job rather than simply pretend we were going to replace the flooring in a room and calculate the number of square feet needed.

Colored Paper Better Than White

I am a big fan of colored paper and high-liters. An abundance of white space confuses me. In my mind, white areas on the paper represent open spaces—spaces that you can get behind or beside. That may sound odd to the average person, but to a 3-dimensional thinker it is normal. Remember nothing is flat (one dimensional) for me. In fact, if you take a magnifying glass and look at your handwriting, you have the same view of writing I do. Writing has high spots, low spots, wide spaces, and raised edges. Fortunately, colored paper or a colored overlay reduces the problem. Colored highlighters also help. Because of the large amount of light a white background reflects, my processing is overwhelmed. My eyes and brain both experience overload, but colors reduce this sense of being overwhelmed.

Using colored highlighters also help organize my thoughts. I highlight information based on particular types. For example, I often highlight the topic of a paragraph with yellow, key words with blue, and supporting details with green. This allows me to skim written material easily and more effectively. It helps me avoid the pitfalls of feeling that I'm hanging in open space or being distracted by the texture of the letters on the page.

Surprises or Major Changes

I don't like surprises! When you spring a surprise on me, I have to try to figure out the Big Picture of where things are going. I clear my head of previous thoughts and come up with a new visual perception. I research my mind to find the big picture until I visually connect and find it. Oftentimes, though, I can't completely disconnect from my original idea or task. For example, if I'm planning to paint the grill in the back yard and my wife asks me to take out the garbage; I may end up in the back yard painting the trash cans. When two ideas with pictures and concepts overlap, a new activity may transpire.

Rapidly fired questions (multiple questions one after another) push my stress level to an overload point. For example, imagine I am drawing a picture of a fish chasing a worm and I've almost completed the picture. After I have drawn a boat with a fisherman holding his pole over the water and have begun drawing the fish and the worm, you suddenly ask me to change the picture to a dog chasing a cat, so I begin to change things around. Then all of a sudden you tell me just to draw a cat chasing a dog. All of this has happened within a couple of minutes, and I have had to come up with a new visual connection each time the focus changes or a new question is posed.

Every time a new question is asked, it increases the load on my visual imagery, cognitive skills, and auditory skills. If given questions orally, it also taxes my auditory processing, and with that kind of workload my natural fight or flight responses kick in. It took nearly my whole life for me to realize that I have to ask the questioner, "Can we pause so that my mind can catch up with the conversation? If I don't do this, I will be frustrated and mad. It's not that I can't answer your questions or do what you ask, I just can't keep up with the pace and processing it requires."

Summing it Up

You probably think "no wonder he can't learn

anything; this guy is stupid and can't remember anything. How am I supposed to help someone like this?" Or if you have these problems yourself, you may wonder, "How will I achieve and survive?" Trust me, there were days when I wondered the same things, but I have found success. One key to success is accepting and knowing that these challenges exist. Not every student, adult, or individual has the same issues as I do. The problem may be similar or have some variation, but it is necessary to realize that something about the person's learning process is different. The good news is that along with these difficulties, I also have strengths which I will discuss later.

I learned how to work with, live with, and manage these challenges. Although I like things to come in a predictable sequence does not mean I want my life to be predictable. In fact if I leave my house going somewhere I go every day, I usually go a different direction. If I just want to get something done, I use the most familiar and often the shortest path. I do this for a number of reasons. I use the travel time for orientation to the world around me—my neighborhood, my community. This allows me to know what's around the next corner if I need to change directions for some reason. It also allows for additional visual stimulus. This stimulates my brain and allows me time to think about the things that have happened or will happen throughout the day.

You might think planning my day would be better done at home. However, even when I make a "To Do" list at home, I may go off to work and forget that I made the list. Also, when I am at home, there are so many things to do that I start to do one of them but never complete it. I often sit down to make a list of things to do, and then get sidetracked thinking I need to refill my tea glass. I get up to get more tea and see that the coffee pot needs cleaning, so I start cleaning the coffee pot. After that I decide to take a shower and go to bed. Tomorrow this whole process starts all over.

Non-Academic Issues

OTHER ISSUES BESIDES my academic performance also affected my success in school, so I have placed them in a separate category. For example, my lack of well-developed social and life skills made me feel uncomfortable with non-disabled peers. I simply couldn't relax around them or take the risk of trying to develop relationships with them.

Having to choose appropriate reactions and verbal responses was so difficult for me that I was paranoid about how to respond. Although I didn't particularly want to be alone, it was just more comfortable for me. Being around people, especially in public, was so difficult I didn't consider it to be worth the effort. Yet if you had known me at that time, you might have thought I was just shy and socially awkward.

Social Skills

Social skills were especially hard for me. Throughout my public school years I had trouble connecting with people, and there were many reasons for this. I didn't understand normal social cues or the correct protocol for engaging in social situations, and I doubt that anyone ever directly taught social skills to me at home or school.

Part of the problem also could have been my inability to master the basics of communication. I've explained previously how I didn't always correctly hear the individual sounds of words, and this delayed my processing time and hindered my understanding. This in turn sometimes contributed to my inappropriate responses and created situations which convinced me it was better not to respond at all.

My limited engagements with other children when I was younger only added to my difficulty with social skills when I was older. As a teenager, I still could not read social cues or respond appropriately. It wasn't that I was antisocial; I just never learned how to engage well with others. However, I was aware that my younger siblings knew how to make and keep friends. They seemingly were popular at school, but I knew that I definitely wasn't.

Living On An Island

Because of my difficulties with social skills, I built around me what counselors call emotional walls. I avoided getting too close to people, and I tried to be self-sufficient but didn't really succeed. I tried to depend only upon myself as if I lived alone on an island. I also did what I wanted to do when I wanted to do it. I spent a lot of time daydreaming, and I wished for a reality which could never be attained. Yet the truth of the matter is that what I really wanted and needed were friends and relationships. Social isolation delayed my development not only cognitively and mentally, but also socially and emotionally. Because of having spent so much time alone, I lacked opportunities to develop and perfect my emotional skills.

This lack of emotional skills caused embarrassing social situations. For example, when responding to something funny, rather than just snicker, I might carry on with a horse laugh. I also could not adequately judge other people's intentions and body language. When someone showed kindness, I might interpret it as affection. On the other hand, when someone was indifferent toward me, I might interpret it as hatred.

Because of not having developed and practiced these social skills, I created a situation which perpetuated my isolation for years. In my later teens and twenties while struggling to compete and fit in, I turned to drugs and alcohol in order to feel socially acceptable. I used them as my ladder of choice to scale my emotional walls in order to engage with others. Using drugs and alcohol became the only way I knew to fit in.

Mechanical Eyes

Another difference between most other people and me is how I approach many situations in life scientifically; I process things as a mechanic might. For example, when I need to move something heavier than usual, I immediately look for a pulley or lever. I tell people that I tend to work smarter, not harder.

76 • LIVING WITH A LEARNING DIFFERENCE (DISABILITY)

Fortunately, science was never an issue for me except when it involved reading and spelling.

I understand scientific processes well—such as why the form of water changes as it gets colder. I visualize in my mind how water becomes solid when frozen because the molecules can't move. I understand why and how a combustion engine works. I understand the processes which make an air conditioner work by removing heat to cool the air, rather than adding coolness to the air. I know that light changes darkness, not the opposite of that.

I think creatively outside the box but have not always understood how or why I do this. Others may accept such things as toasters without curiosity. However, beginning in childhood, I sought complete understanding of processes in the mechanical devices around me, even toasters. How was bread heated on both sides? How did the mechanism know when to pop the toast out? Because of my reading disability, I couldn't read to find the answers. Therefore, in order to understand how a toaster worked, I had to take it apart.

When I was young, I took apart nearly every mechanical object in my house in order to understand its processes, especially ones which had been thrown away. I took apart vacuum cleaners, saws, drills, can openers—anything with an on and off switch. Fans were my favorite. I also loved to take apart and fix transistor radios and tube radios. Consequently, I received quite a few electrical shocks, and that is probably why I am not afraid of electricity even now.

My first car was a '54 Chevrolet, and I loved it. I

changed its color multiple times, and I took the body parts off and then put them back on. I took the interior out, changed the voltage system, changed the transmission from standard to an automatic, changed the column shift to a floor shift, took out the windows, replaced the glass in the windows, and put them back in. My dad wouldn't let me take the motor apart, but when it needed work I went under the car with the mechanic.

My car was 23 years old, and after a couple of years it couldn't withstand my taking it apart and then putting it back together. My second vehicle was a 13-year-old pickup. I also learned everything about it, installed an oversize carburetor, and took off the bed in order to make it a flatbed. However, removing its motor unfortunately ended my Chevrolet's life.

Ultimately, this huge hunger to understand mechanical processes turned out to be important at school, also. My mechanical skills eventually helped open the door a little for me to make progress in school work. Finally, I had some, though limited, academic success during my public school years.

Common Sense; But Not So Common

With the combination of my lack of social skills, my mechanical processing, and my excessive period of isolation, I failed to develop what many people refer to as common sense. Webster defines common sense as good sound judgment. It represents what most people agree that an average person should do in a typical situation. Common sense is not to be confused with intelligence. My lack of common sense was a combination of a lack of experience, unique thought processes, and personal evaluations of my experiences. Common sense might better be referred to as common knowledge, and it is now often called "street smarts."

Normally people do not walk off and leave their cars unlocked with the keys still in the ignition but I did not normally remember to consider everything like that. I was so focused on what I was trying to accomplish, I neglected other important things. For example, once when I worked on a fan, I immediately tore into it without unplugging the fan.

The use of common sense requires that a person process more than one thing at a time. You need to hold in your mind what you want to do as well as to evaluate all possible outcomes. For example, before taking out a load-bearing wall in a home, one must consider what other supports the ceiling and roof will have in order to keep them from sagging. Removing a wall also affects doors and sheet-rock, so that requires additional advance planning. For this example, of course, knowledge of building principles is needed as well as common sense.

On the Brain, Out the Mouth

My problem with saying things before thinking them through probably relates to a lack of common sense, but I think it also deserves its own category. It is important to know when not to respond as well how to respond. Unfortunately when I was younger, I didn't always think about things before saying them.

For example, when I was in high school, a group

of youth from our church went on a trip to Austin on a Saturday. During the following Sunday morning service, the pastor announced that one of the younger youth had arrived shortly after the group had left and was sorely disappointed that she didn't get to go. He indicated that we acted irresponsibly to have left without her. I immediately stood up and let the pastor know that the young girl was aware of the time we were leaving and should have been there on time. Now I realize how terribly inappropriate it was to do this during a Sunday morning worship service. Unfortunately this was neither the first nor the last outburst of saying exactly what was on my mind.

Another connection between my saying and thinking is that I need to write down important thoughts or say them to someone aloud before I forget what I am thinking. Also, for most of my speaking engagements and lectures in class, I begin thinking of what I will say well in advance. Once I start speaking, I am somewhat unaware of what is coming out of my mouth, because I am so focused on covering the material I have already prepared in my mind well in advance of actually saying it.

When I'm asked to speak about something that I have not had time to practice in my mind, I may be less organized, speak less intelligently, and sound less professional than when I have time to process it first in my mind. To deal with this situation, I tend to focus on my areas of expertise and anticipate what questions might be asked. I then practice responses or appropriate remarks in my mind. I often think out loud and talk through these processes to myself. I have learned when asked a question that I often need to respond with "I will get back with you on that." I know I will need time to think through it in order to compose an intelligent, professional response.

Strengths

SOME THINGS YOU cannot change, yet all of the issues we previously discussed can eventually become strengths. Being "learning different" does not mean that a person is altogether different from what is considered normal. My experience as an adult having post-secondary academic success suggests that optimistic outcomes are real possibilities for individuals with similar struggles. Although there are some things I cannot change, I have a number of strengths upon which I can build. For starters, I have average intelligence (an IQ score over 100). That means I am not stupid, but neither am I gifted. However, there are some areas in which I excel more than others normally do.

Visualization

The first strength is my strong visual memory, and it is very important to my creative efforts and success. Since I visualize what I want to do, I can physically copy it in my mind. For example, when I was ready to go to college, I needed to increase my vocabulary.

I was told by a friend who understands children with language disorders that in order to expand my vocabulary I needed to be around individuals who used a higher level vocabulary. This was not a novel idea, but the process with which I increased my vocabulary was novel. It involved my making visual images of the individuals who spoke these new words. Basically what I did was watch, listen, and then visually imagine myself using the words I heard.

Another example of my use of visualization occurred while working my way through college. I worked on air as a radio personality for a country radio show. When I first became an on-air personality, it was difficult to know what to say. In order to improve my speaking skills, I began to listen to other radio personalities on my way to work and then visually imagine myself saying and doing what they said and did. By using more than one personality as my model, I began to blend their activities and verbal responses to create my own style.

That on-air speaking skill later became the skill I transformed into my public speaking career and also the lecture style I use to teach college courses. Before every speaking engagement or lecture, I must take time to imagine or visualize which parts of the material I will cover, what I will say, and sometimes even how the audience will respond. Through visualization I am able to reduce stress, increase my speaking efficiency, and make better connections to convey the message I want to deliver. Without the visualization process, I think I might return to incoherent unconnected thoughts.

Strong Memory

I have the ability to recite in a very coherent manner when I have time to practice. I have a great memory for storytelling and remembering colorful details from family events and activities. I am able to memorize directions and details of places I have been, even if I have only been there once. I have an excellent recollection of personal experiences and details, funny facts, and feelings associated with particular personal experiences.

My listening comprehension is much higher than my reading comprehension. Even though I read slowly, I am still able to retain a large portion of what I read, however. Whether listening or reading, I must formulate all concepts and ideas into visual images. Once I visualize these concepts and ideas, I always remember them. It's as if I've taken miniature pictures or short movies which I can recall with ease.

I never realized this in my younger years. I'm not sure if I possessed this skill in my early years or if I developed it later in life. However, I do remember some things from my childhood very vividly. By developing and utilizing these methods to remember, my success in school and in life improved greatly.

I also believe these skills fuel my creative problem-solving abilities. Creativity is linked with my personal memories and what I do every day. Past details help me recognize or predict what individuals will probably do or how events may transpire.

I Notice Things

I am very mindful of what I am doing and how it

relates to my preferred outcomes. I notice things which others fail to consider and may actually choose to ignore. This ability is also a source of creativity. In fact, this conscious consideration of details often provides an insight into a problem which no one else has discovered before. Also, the things I notice may also trigger in my mind a different way of doing things which is more effective.

This visualization process is how I form a picture or a solid concept of complex issues. For example, when I travel to a new location to speak, I don't know the type or size of room where I will speak until I get there. In order not to be thrown off by something in the room, I try to arrive early. When possible I will even go a day early so that I have time to see and get comfortable with the place where I will speak. This allows me to identify potential problems or any other issues. Once I see a problem, I'm able to quickly sort through it and find a solution.

Big Picture Thinking

Once I find the forest (the big picture), I visually compare it to other areas and concepts which have similar connections. My visual memory images are much easier to sort through to identify and to recall than auditory information. Images allow me to own the big picture or concept.

There was a time when I was fairly good at drawing very complex details of vehicles or trucks. In fact I had a short career in automotive paint and body. I painted cars and trucks and added striping on them. I could visualize the concept of the paint job and then create it. I even worked with murals. I could sketch out objects such as houses, cars, and flowers, but that never became a real passion. Because of my ability to focus on small parts within the larger picture, I often have a heightened sense for details, and these details greatly interest me.

Mechanically Minded

Mechanically inclined is a phrase used to describe someone who is very good at building or fixing things like cars, computers, small electronics, household appliances, etc. As a mechanically inclined individual, I am able to visualize complex systems without getting frustrated, and these results in strong critical thinking skills. It also means I am able to look at a machine, visualize in my mind the parts or pieces in the mechanics, and determine what it will take to fix, alter, or improve the item.

Because of my mechanical strengths, I've learned to see everything, including my academic work, as a mechanical problem requiring a mechanical process. I write sentences based on number of words derived from bulletin thoughts. Paragraphs have about five sentences and nearly every paper has three main sections with five sub-parts in each section. Every paper I write is a presentation that I imagine I am giving. So when someone asks, "How do you overcome your problems?" My answer is "By building on your strengths."

III. Resilience

Finding Competence to recover strength and spirit under adversity on both internal (self) and external (family, school, community) factors

Nikao

THE WORD NIKAO (/Knee/ /Cow/) is a Greek word that means to overcome or conquer. To overcome, according to the dictionary, means **to deal with successfully or to win the case.** However, I prefer to define it as **to conquer** through physical, emotional, and spiritual toughness. Individuals with learning differences must believe that it is possible to strengthen oneself through resilience (Werner, 1999).

Research and experience supports the fact that 25% to 35% of students enter school with factors which place them at risk of failing socially and academically (Sameroff, Seifer, Baldwin, and Baldwin, 1993). For that reason many educators falsely assume that these risk factors make it impossible for such students to succeed in school and in life. However, some of these students later develop characteristics which will help them overcome their learning challenges and give them the important attributes of strength and resilience.

Resilience

I see the term resilience as not representing a personality trait but rather a construct or concept that implies there are factors within each of use that will foster a positive adjustment and outcome when negative challenges arise. Resilience is a process where an individual displays positive adaptation despite experiences of significant adversity. Studies on resilience have found a place in research, and now resiliency is identified as a valuable research topic (Rutter, 2001; Masten, 1994).

In Dr. Emmy Werner's longitudinal study of high-risk individuals (1999), she found that individuals identified as more successful in life usually had received emotional support from family members as well as support from community members, ministers, and teachers. She found that these individuals possessed strong capabilities and context beliefs, responded well to positive influences, and were more oriented toward achievement. Dr Werner followed a group of 22 individuals (13 boys, 9 girls) with learning difficulties from birth to age 32 years in an effort to identify the factors that led some to have successful coping skills in early adulthood. Results of the study identified a cluster of factors that served to promote positive outcomes for this group of individuals. These factors included:

1. Positive responses from others
2. Efficient use of personal abilities including confidence that the odds could be overcome
3. Realistic educational and vocational plans,
4. Regular home responsibilities (everyday jobs)

5. Care-giving styles that reflected competence and promoted self-esteem in the child
6. Supportive adults who acted as gatekeepers for the future
7. Opportunities that set a positive course to adulthood.

So let's look at the two sides of the resilience coin: those who need help and those who provide help. Resilient individuals learn to use specific resources to accommodate and overcome encountered risks (whether physical, emotional, or spiritual). Some researchers in the field have devoted their time to establish commonalities among those individuals who are educationally resilient and therefore beat the odds against them and obtain positive life outcomes (Werner, 1999; Miller & Fritz, 1998). Educational resiliency among specific groups, such as individuals with learning difficulties, is still an area which needs to be investigated more deeply. Since resiliency is a timely and important topic and a key to my success, I feel I must examine the characteristics of resiliency as they pertain to my Nikao. We will look at how to develop within ourselves physical buoyancy, emotional plasticity, and spiritual character. All of these will be discussed in the chapters to come.

Fostering Resilience

For the remainder of this chapter let's talk about what you as a teacher, parent, or friend can do to help an individual with a disability. Helping students develop and increase their resiliency is an excellent way to strengthen and give them hope when they might otherwise stop trying. In order to do this, teachers or parents need to understand the definition of resilience and also become acquainted with current research in this field. Once factors contributing to resilience are identified, this knowledge must then be applied when teaching students. As we explore and develop skills in this area, we will eventually be able to help many more students with learning difficulties to become resilient, also.

To help foster resilience in individuals with a disability, you first must care for them as individuals. Teachers who develop positive relationships with students convey the message that their students are loved unconditionally and that they are important. Cultivating within students a feeling of acceptance actually helps meet their basic survival needs. This type of teacher/student connection also translates into their feeling emotionally safe in our presence. In order to accomplish this, however, we must routinely look beyond poor behavior or performance in order to determine whether struggling students or individuals are already doing their best. After all, that is the most you can reasonably expect from them.

It is also necessary to avoid negativity. Negative comments leave the impression that you see these students in a negative light, and individuals with physical and academic difficulties then feel defective. Negative body language and comments directed toward an individual with difficulties is perceived by others as directly related to capabilities and worthiness of the individual. Continued negative body language and comments toward the struggling individual will increase the likelihood that their peers will view them as inferior or as a problem.

You must monitor what you say to and about struggling individuals. Make it a habit to say something positive in every bad situation. When individual students perform poorly, take time to find something good to say about them in order to reduce the stress of their less than perfect responses, written work, and/or behavior. Finding something good in every situation will help struggling individuals learn to respond better to loss, change, major illness, or any of life's other challenges.

Help struggling individuals learn to trust their instincts (their inner voice or gut feelings) as a primary guide. For example, when I play golf, I have an unpleasant hook. In order to correct for the hook, I turn my body and use it to get the ball where I want it to go. When you make decisions based on inner instincts, it may not be perfect but you begin to understand how you think and then you can adjust your responses based on previous outcomes. Another personal example is that when I prepare a presentation or lecture, my inner instinct gives me an estimate of how much time it will take (for example, 4 hours). However, I know from past experience that it always takes me twice as much time as I expected. Therefore I know I will actually need 8 hours to prepare. My instincts are not perfect, but they are useful.

Most learning disabled individuals struggle with this

at first, but they will improve and then will not be unduly influenced by what others expect. It is useful for them to become "level"—to find a middle ground—in their expectations. When expectations are too high, a person feels less successful, feels more out of control, and may even give up. On the other hand, one should never accept as an ultimate goal a less than acceptable product. For example, teach your students to think of this process of leveling as a ladder on which you take one step at a time in order to reach the top.

As a teacher, parent, or friend, if you are not sure about where to set expectations for them, try to remember yourself at that age, and also compare the struggling student's behavior or performance to that of their peers. In addition, you may ask parents with non-struggling individuals about their children's behavior. All of this information will help you better help struggling students set appropriate goals.

Help struggling individuals identify a purpose in life, in school, in the community, etc. According to Abraham Maslow (author of Maslow's Hierarchy of Needs), purpose is one of the key elements that individuals must have. For struggling individuals, having a purpose is a somewhat overwhelming concept. The easiest way to explain purpose is to talk to them about the big picture, about the world outside the home and classroom, about considering others, about making a difference. Encourage them by helping them see that they have choices. In every situation, every person has a choice about what to do and how to respond.

Help struggling individual master basic skills. Good systematic direct instruction will help them improve in the areas of art, sports, math, reading, dancing, music, languages, drama, spelling and other areas which challenge them. This helps them develop skills as well as identify areas where accommodations may be needed. As a result of direct instruction, students also learn that they are good at doing some of these things which will help them develop positive feelings and confidence. In addition, struggling individuals might discover that they really enjoy certain subjects which may lead them to continue to improve in these areas. When individuals are good at something, they experience success and get positive feedback from their peers. For struggling students, achievements as a result of their hard work will motivate them to keep moving forward even when they have difficulties

Another useful activity is to teach struggling individuals to be flexible. Flexible individuals adjust well to different ideas and changing situations. Teach them to try different kinds of food, have them listen to different kinds of music, and expose them to different cultures, different social groups, and different hobbies. Through such opportunities, struggling individuals learn to understand and experience the rewards of taking positive risks.

When struggling individuals continually blame others or their circumstances for poor outcomes, they fail to develop personal power over their lives. Provide them opportunities to be inspired. Expose them to inspiring people who have won against all odds. Tell or read to them real stories about successful people (artists, business people, actors, singers, etc.) who overcame their obstacles and difficulties. Also identify and tell them personal stories from your life that reveal how you recovered from hard experiences.

Physical Buoyancy

FOR INDIVIDUALS WITH a disability such as I have, the first thing they must learn is to ask for help. This was by far one of the hardest things I had to do. As a male, I enjoy being independent. I didn't then (and still don't) like to ask for help or ask for directions. However, in order to move past my obstacles in reading and writing, I had to learn to ask for help and to understand that just because something was wrong, not everything was wrong.

While having a psychological exam in 1992 at the age of 33, I was formally diagnosed with two distinct learning disabilities. The truth is, by this time, I had already begun to understand that there was a problem and I needed some help, although I was still uncomfortable asking for it. For example, I would drop my boys off at the corner or a block away from the elementary school in order to avoid any situation where I might have to write a note for one of my boys or read and sign a document. My self-esteem was so fragile that any such disclosure outside of my control created panic and fear.

After receiving information from the psychologist, I wanted to know more about learning disabilities and to get information from people I knew who might understand my problems. One of the first individuals I talked to was my rehabilitation caseworker, Susan Arnold, who had a master's degree in English. Although she didn't know a lot about learning disabilities, she quickly picked up on the difficulties I was having and suggested the use of assistive technology. Texas Rehabilitation Commission and Susan helped me get a computer which had memory, a hard drive, and simple text-document software. Perhaps the best thing Susan told me was that if I didn't ask for help, I wouldn't get it.

Next, I had to seek out experts. Susan Reeves, my neighbor, was a speech pathologist with West Texas Rehabilitation Center. She had a unique understanding of processing issues, speech problems, and language development in young children. Susan became a valued resource as I began to explore my academic issues and challenges. She provided a foundation for me to understand some of my difficulties in spelling. She also encouraged me to overcome my insecurity by writing ideas on paper without worrying whether the words were spelled correctly. Then I could go back to identify my mistakes and focus on areas in the document which needed changing rather than on the personal issues which inhibited my performance. She told me that many children and adults have these issues, also. Fortunately, most problems of this type are now addressed earlier in schools or in the Rehab Center with the help of a therapist. The fact that I was in my 30s didn't mean that I couldn't correct many of them, but it might take more work than if I were younger.

I had to learn to ask for specific help. First I sought help from my wife Arlene. She had never really understood my academic issues. (She struggles to figure them out even today.) However, she was willing to encourage me, tutor me, read to me, write for me, and type for me when I needed it most. As a man and as the provider for my family, it was hard to ask her for help. I actually had to learn how to ask. I didn't want someone to do it for me, but I desperately needed assistance in specific areas of need. For example, when I first started to try to improve my writing, I would ask my wife to proofread what I wrote. My wife was an "A" student and debated the merits of her work with a passion. However, as she will tell you, she is not a teacher. So, when she corrected my paper, she would rephrase, rearrange, and restructure it to be the paper she would write. Unfortunately, it might have been a good paper, but it was not my voice, and, in most cases, I didn't understand what she had written. What I really needed was to identify things that I had done wrong and then be taught how to correct them. It took many years for my wife to understand that I didn't need if rewritten, I needed specific appropriate help.

Over the years, I have built a network of individuals whom I can ask for help with my disability issues. Many of these individuals are friends who assist me because they care; others are colleagues with whom

I trade editing services for technology or instructional assistance. Others are individuals that I pay for their services. In fact on my dissertation I hired an AP editor who helped me by discussing verb tense, word choices, and the context of confusing sentences and paragraphs. She never changed my voice or my writing style but helped me convey in an appropriate manner the information I needed to share.

The truth is we all need help with something. It may be with writing, spelling, or reading, but it could just as easily be with settings on the TV or DVD or DVR, changing the vacuum cleaner belt, changing the filter on an ice maker, or setting up a spreadsheet in Microsoft Excel. Individuals who are resilient learn that when they need help, they should ask for help. This is not done to avoid work, but to obtain assistance when assistance is needed. They learn that they have strengths, and they may trade or barter with those strengths to get assistance in areas where they have difficulties. Assistance can be solicited from close family members, friends, or others who are willing to help. Accepting help and support from those who care about you and who will listen to you strengthens your resilience.

Take Care of Yourself

Individuals with disabilities often strongly feel that they are overworked and challenged too much by the demands of a job, family, and the rest of life. Let me start by saying you are not alone. Yet, as an individual with disabilities, this often seems more than anyone should have to tolerate, but we can handle it by learning to carve the challenges up in to small manageable parts.

You can't always control the circumstances that life throws your way, but if you take care of yourself, you can control how you respond. Taking care of yourself is one of the most important things you can do. It helps keep your mind and body primed to deal with situations requiring resilience. Practicing this type of self-care can help you see problems as a challenge rather than a threat. Also, taking care of your own needs and maintaining healthy habits will help you keep your reserves up and allow you to feel more in control of your life.

Being prepared to handle problems enables you to be proactive rather when dealing with them instead of just reacting to them. This could mean asking family members and friends to help out with major challenges or passing some work-related projects over to a co-worker.

In order to achieve a balance in your life in the areas of work, family, friends, and rest, you need a plan. When planning, make it a point to schedule time for the following: taking a personal day, developing relationships, celebrating accomplishments, exercising your body, relaxing your mind, and renewing your spirit. Regarding myself, I know that if it is not on the calendar, then it probably will not happen. I am not telling you that you need to change your whole life, but I am saying you need to reduce the stress in your life, and these activities will help you reduce it.

I have learned that everyone at some point needs to **take a personal day**. But as an individual with a learning disability, it is even more important. When you spend five or more work days out of the week on your job, occasionally you need a break. It is important to take a personal day and forget your responsibilities for just that one day. It helps to put away your "to do list" and revel in all the things you like to do but shouldn't. You might need to let your desk stay unorganized and your house or room be messy, sleep in, eat an ice-cream sundae for supper, and watch a movie. (I especially enjoy funny movies with no major plot, even stupid ones.) Put on a favorite CD and dance! Let the little kid in you come out and play!

Learn to relax and clear the mind. Stop the chaos and take a break. Schedule a day on the calendar just for you. Promise yourself to enjoy time off. Turn off the computer, and don't answer the phone. Don't let guilt or a list of impending deadlines steal your relaxation and enjoyment during this day that you so desperately need. **Celebrate your accomplishments** and treat yourself to a night out. This is a special time that the whole family should look forward to. Even God took a break on the seventh day. (See Genesis 2:2 in the Bible.)

Exercise your body, don't just be a couch potato. Head to the gym, take a walk in the park, get on the treadmill, or take a dip in the pool. Take in a game of golf, racquetball or tennis; exercise is a proven stress reducer! Get outside, there's nothing more energizing than feeling the sunshine on your face and perspiring a little. Spend time in your garden, play ball with the kids, or take a trip to the park. Work in the backyard by digging around the flowers and trees. Even one-on-one basketball is fun with a neighbor. Increased blood flow stimulates the brain and increases cognition. In other words, you will think more efficiently.

You need to understand relationships are important. We were designed by God to need others. **Develop relationships** with close friends or get reacquainted with old friends. Go on a date with your spouse. Enjoy a cup of gourmet coffee with a friend and talk about the things you have in common. Steal away on a father/daughter or father/son evening, trip, or adventure. Write a special note to a friend or spouse letting them know how you feel about them. Give someone special a long meaningful non-sexual hug. Spend a little extra time cuddling with your kiddos before bed time. Close relationships allow you to feel connected to the great cosmos, plus family and friends can be your greatest cheerleaders.

Often in the busyness of life, we forget to take quiet time for ourselves. I encourage you to **relax your mind and renew your spirit.** Take time to journal, daydream, read scriptures, and meditate. Take time to turn off the busy work and focus on what is really important to you. Go to church and be inspired, join a Bible study and discover a greater sense of value. Take time to listen to your heart, reflect and honor the quiet voice within. Indulge yourself with a soak in the hot tub or a bubble bath. Listen to your favorite soothing music. Read a great novel. Soak up some sun at the beach or take a day at the spa. Whatever you choose, keep life in balance. "*All work and no play*" is not good; however, "*all play and no work*" will leave you unemployed.

Develop Realistic Goals

Ask yourself, "What is one thing I know I can accomplish today to help me move in the direction I want to go?" I encourage you to write down the goals you want to reach. Your goals should be straightforward and should emphasize what you want to happen. **Specific goals** help focus your efforts and clearly define what you are going to do. I encourage you to write these goals down and review them regularly. Ensure that your goals are very specific, clear, and reasonable. Instead of setting a goal to lose weight and be healthier, set specific goals to lose 20 pounds and run 2 miles at a specific pace.

I would suggest using the SMART mnemonics for goals. When developing your goals you want to keep these 5 points in mind:
1. **S**pecific - easily understood and unambiguous
2. **M**easurable - a way to determine when the goal is attained
3. **A**ttainable - not too easy and yet not too difficult
4. **R**elevant - relevant to your particular needs and abilities
5. **T**ime bound - must have specific dates for completion.

"Specific" includes the What, Why, and How of the goal. When you talk about **what** be sure to use action words such as direct, organize, coordinate, lead, develop, plan, build, etc. Add to this **why** it is important to complete this task at this time. Describe what it is and why it is you ultimately want to accomplish this. Be sure you include the steps for **how** to accomplish the goal.

If you can't **measure** it, you can't verify that the goal has been accomplished. In the broadest sense, the goal statement as a whole becomes the measure for the project and determines when it is completed. This overall goal is normally constructed of several smaller goals with short-term measurements that are built into the primary goal. Each measured short-term goal is a step toward the major goal and becomes a reason to celebrate. Developing and establishing concrete criteria for measuring progress toward the attainment of each goal will allow you to stay on track. Be sure you understand and research a reasonable target and date for attaining it.

Be specific when you set your goals. Set a goal such as "I want to write this book, and I need to write one chapter per month this year. I want to complete it by August 30th." (This was one of my specific target goals.) Specific goals allow you to measure progress throughout the project. A goal such as "I want to write a book" is not specific or measurable enough to keep most people on track to reach it.

When you identify a goal, you must first determine if it is attainable, or better yet, ask yourself if there is anything that would make the goal unattainable. Determine the steps or events you must accomplish in order to make the goal come true. Next, determine if there is anything which might prevent you from obtaining the goal. Ask yourself whether after you have developed the attitudes, abilities, skills, and financial capability to reach the goal there could still be something else to stop you. Also, look for previously overlooked opportunities to bring yourself closer to achieving your goal.

Keep your goals and focus within your reach. Goals that are too far off or out of your reach will not keep you motivated, and you will probably not be committed to obtaining them. Although you may have the best of intentions, the knowledge that it's too great for you means your subconscious will stop you from giving it your best. A goal needs to stretch you slightly but allow you to feel you can reach it with sufficient commitment.

For challenging long-term goals, use small goals to move you in the right direction until the large goal becomes just another small goal. For instance, if you want to lose 100 lbs. in 5 years, that can be achieved, but most of us won't stay motivated that long. However, by setting a goal to lose 1 lb. per week and achieving that goal weekly for a year proves that it is achievable and keeps you motivated. Attaining a weekly goal also brings feelings of success and keeps you inspired.

Keep your goal setting realistic—in other words, "do-able." It means that the learning curve is not a vertical slope. Also, the skills you need to do the work are available, and the project fits well with your overall strategy for life. A realistic goal may push you to improve your skills and knowledge, but it shouldn't break you. The goal of never again eating German Chocolate Cake is not realistic for me because I enjoy it immensely. It would be more realistic for me to say I won't eat more than five pieces of German Chocolate Cake per year. Or I might set a goal of eating a piece of fruit every other time instead of eating cake whenever I want. I can then choose to work towards a gradual reduction of the amount of German Chocolate Cake I eat.

Be sure you don't just set simple goals that you can attain with very little effort. If your goals are too difficult you set the stage for failure, but if they are too easy it sends a subconscious message that you aren't capable of achieving anything big. Carefully set your goals high enough for satisfying achievement.

In addition to weekly goals, identify an end point for reaching your goal in order to have a clear target to work towards. Without a set time for completion, your commitment may not be strong enough to reach the finish line. Also, without a time limit, there's no urgency even to start taking action. An expected end point also helps you assess your progress toward reaching the goal.

Take Decisive Actions

One of the most destructive things we usually do is to procrastinate. Procrastination elevates stress and decreases motivation. A common factor with individuals who are depressed is procrastination. That is not to say you should make rash decisions. Instead, you should devise a plan and take decisive action, and that's where goal setting plays a key factor. Until you understand where you're going, it's hard to make good decisions. Individuals with disabilities often have a history of poor decision making. Our decisions are poor because we often do not fully understand what we want to accomplish or what the end result should be. To avoid making poor decisions, we must clearly understand both our abilities and disabilities—what we can and cannot do. For example; writing this book is not something I can do without help. I can think of what needs to be included, but I'm not the one who can clean it up and make it publishable. So to write this book, I had to identify someone who could edit it and make the text more presentable. The longer I procrastinated in identifying and securing that person, the more doubtful I became that the book would ever be written.

Goals help define where you want to go or what you want to accomplish. All decisions should be based on those goals. Failure to align your decisions with your goals creates confusion, confusion creates stress, and stress reduces productivity. Every time a decision or situation comes up, I have to rely upon the goals I have previously set in order to arrive at that answer. I take time to weigh pros and cons, but ultimately I need to make a decision. That doesn't mean I always make the right decision, but there is nothing wrong in changing a decision when necessary. Failure to act becomes a coping mechanism which prevents positive movement. On the other hand, resilience involves maintaining flexibility and balance in life in order to handle stressful circumstances and traumatic events successfully.

Emotional Plasticity

IN A LETTER to the Thessalonians, Paul wrote to encourage them as a young church. One of the statements he made to this church is that God is in control and His will ensures a good outcome. (First Thessalonians 5:18 says, "Be thankful in all circumstances, for this is God's will for you who belong to Christ Jesus.") One of the harder lessons in life that I had to learn is that sometimes I have to be unsuccessful in order for God to be successful. One country song notes, "Thank God for unanswered prayer," and that may be what some think, but actually all prayers are answered. Sometimes, however, the answer is "No." In the bigger picture of life which we often cannot see, God ultimately has a plan, and He continues to use difficult situations as opportunities to help us grow.

Likewise, in the book of Romans, Paul again expresses that God is in control and His will works to our advantage. (Romans 8:28 tells us "And we know that in all things God works for the good of those who love Him, who have been called according to his purpose.")

Although you can't stop stressful events from happening, you can change how you interpret and respond to these events. The truth is, every obstacle is a learning opportunity, although sometimes we will not understand immediately what we need to gain or learn from it. The main truth to remember during these times is that there is a reason, and in time we may understand it. Even when we don't understand, that's OK, too.

Early obstacles in my life have been opportunities to expand my understanding of learning challenges, dysfunctional families, and emotional issues. Much of what any of us learn will take place in the presence of failure. I like to use the following analogy in many of my presentations: "Natural athletes seldom make the best coaches." Great coaches are people who have struggled to learn the process, have identified needed skills and techniques, and have personally learned how to use those skills and techniques to succeed. The same is true of many individuals who are successful teachers/leaders in their field. They have personally had to discover the essence of their area. My struggle with academics has made me more sensitive to the issues of children who have to struggle to learn.

My personal struggles with reading provided me the opportunity to understand all the components of reading and to develop the skills needed to teach reading. However, even though I have the necessary skills to teach reading doesn't mean that I have complete mastery of all reading skills myself. So just like a good coach. I understand the concepts and requirements of necessary skills even though I did not personally excel in all of them. When I coach football, I understand the responsibilities of an offensive lineman even though I played defense. I was never a good offensive lineman myself, but I can teach someone who has the necessary physical ability how to be an effective offensive linemen. Teaching well and doing something well are separate things.

To align this section with the previous chapter about goal setting, it is important to track or identify areas which seem to be the most challenging. I often look for repeated patterns of stressful events or situations in my own life since these normally signal obstacles in my life. Once those obstacles are identified, I like to incorporate some of those into my personal quiet time and normally use my mornings for reflecting on the past day's activities as well as the present day's activities.

I reflect over the previous day and ask myself what was positive, what didn't work, and what caused me frustration. I then ponder what it was that made some things work and what prevented my success in others. I don't normally have problems remembering what was positive, although remembering exactly what happened might elude me. The difficult part is evaluating things that didn't go the way I would have preferred. For these events I have to ask myself what caused them to go wrong, what would have been a preferred outcome, and how did a lack of skills contribute to the less than successful outcome?

The next focal point after evaluating all of these is to ask what skills I still need to gain knowledge to prevent inappropriate outcomes from happening again. I would like to say that this is an easy process, but that would be misleading. Unfortunately there are still patterns of negative events in my life which I have not yet been able to prevent; therefore, inappropriate outcomes still occasionally happen. Specific obstacles which continue to resurface in my life are difficulties with decoding/reading and encoding/spelling. As I reflect upon these difficulties, I understand that because I have a learning disability, my reading and spelling skills will likely never match that of a non-learning disabled person.

On the other hand, because of these differences and obstacles, I've learned new strategies for reading and spelling and am able to share them with others who have similar problems. I have also learned to be patient with students who struggle with these problems. Additionally, I help teachers view these problems with a different attitude or perspective. Had it not been for my learning obstacles, these opportunities would not exist.

Understanding That Change Is a Normal Part of Life

Accepting circumstances which cannot be changed helps you focus on circumstances which you can alter. A counselor once told me that all change causes pain; it is not relevant whether the change is good or bad. Examples of possible pain are found in the following choices you might have to make if you win the lottery. How should you spend the money and how should you invest it? Should you form a corporation or help extended family members or even let them know you won? Talk about stress! The same situation would occur if you had to file bankruptcy. Which people should you choose to pay? Will you ask someone for help? Will you tell family or friends? These are extreme circumstances, but they reflect how change causes stressful situations.

With all of that being a given, you must understand that nothing stays the same. Think how life is different now than it was 5 years ago, 10 years ago, and 15 or 20 years ago if you can think back that far. Life is constantly changing. Not only do circumstances change, we change, also. We should grow physically, mentally, and spiritually. If you are not growing in these ways, that in itself will cause problems since everyone around you is changing. Although you might isolate yourself to some extent and prevent yourself from making certain changes, you can't completely avoid change in life. For individuals with disabilities (and sometimes for those who don't have them), this fact of change often seems cruel. We struggle so hard to make adjustments to fit in with others and make social and emotional connections only to discover that everything continues to change.

Don't misunderstand me, I don't like change either. Most of us usually prefer comfortable situations—in other words, we like our ruts. But I have learned that since change usually happens, I prefer to be proactive than reactive. I also like to prepare myself as much as I can for upcoming changes. When a change comes that I haven't anticipated, I remind myself that it will take longer the first few times to do whatever is needed in order to complete the task.

Every year I deal with incoming freshmen at the college level, and one thing I tell them is "You're going to get homesick, and you will go home but it will not alleviate the homesick feeling. You're not really longing for your hometown; rather, you are longing for the comfort of your old routine. Cycles in life come to most people every 3 to 7 years. Some experts say the cycles are 5 to 10 years. Whichever cycle it is for you, you need to embrace the fact that life changes."

Sometimes during my work in pastoral counseling, I see individuals who have been married from 5 to 15 years, and one or both have resisted evolving or changing as the relationship changes. As my past experience suggests, relationships go through a major restructuring about every 7 years. Couples who do not take the time to evolve with the relationship often find each other going in different directions. It is not uncommon to hear one or both say "I'm doing exactly what I've always done." However, both individuals have changed to some extent. If they've had children, the children are now older. If the children are grown, the couple may now have grandchildren. These experiences require new responses from them, whether they realize it or not.

If you've had a job which hasn't changed in 15 years, or you haven't been promoted (that is a different conversation), at least your job performance should have changed as you become more effective. Ask yourself, is it truly the same job or has it evolved? In order to be resilient, you must embrace the fact that everything eventually changes. The only option for change not to happen is when you no longer are alive. For this reason, I now accept change as a good thing!

Maintaining an Optimistic Outlook

Your attitude will determine how you respond to obstacles. According to Webster's Dictionary, the word "attitude" means an internal position or feeling with regard to something else. Other words often used as synonyms for attitude are: disposition, feeling, mood, opinion, sentiment, temper, tone, perspective, frame of mind, outlook, view, and morale. Try visualizing what you want, rather than worrying about what you fear. If you know change is coming, accept that it provides you an opportunity for personal, emotional, and/or spiritual growth. When you see change happening, embrace it. Be optimistic and be positive about having change in your life. It means you are growing and maturing. You have the opportunity to be more effective, efficient, and useful. If you embrace change with a positive attitude, you likely will see positive things come from it. It may not be completely pleasant or exactly what you want; nevertheless, it is a chance for you to grow.

In the Bible in Colossians, Paul told church members what it takes to be a good bond servant. In Colossians 3:23-24 he said, "Work willingly at whatever you do, as though you were working for the Lord rather than for people. Remember that the Lord will give you an inheritance as your reward, and that the Master you are serving is Christ." Basically Paul is saying, have a good attitude and do good work in whatever you are doing—at your job, in your home, for your neighbor, and all the things you do.

When I am happy or positive about what I'm doing, the quality of what I do tends to be better, and therefore I take pride in what I have done which strengthens my self-worth and self-esteem. On the other hand, if I'm mad and half-way do something, I may have to do it again which tends to produce feelings of worthlessness and frustration. If you are an individual with learning disabilities like me, you have probably faced this already.

Taking Care of Yourself

Taking care of yourself helps to keep your mind and body primed to deal with situations which require resilience. Part of being ready for and adapting to change with a positive attitude is being physically, mentally, and spiritually healthy. However, any of these three can become a full-time obsession. The real key is to keep them in balance.

Physical exercise (for the sake of doing exercise) is not my favorite pastime. In fact, doing my morning walk outside or on a treadmill is often drudgery. You can tell by looking at me that I came from peasant stock. I am short, stocky, and pudgy, and for all practical purposes I resemble other members of my family. Genetically it may be the way I will always look. The real question is whether additional physical activity will change my overall health. My doctor and my wife would say a resounding "Yes." So I continue to work toward better health. Mind you, better looks and a thinner body are not my ultimate goals. Instead, my goal is better health and a longer life.

For your physical help I suggest you start by doing a moving activity every day, whether it's walking, running, strength training, sports, activities with your family or a friend, or whatever else works for you. If you do that, you will become healthier over time. Start by simply walking 15 to 20 minutes a day and then work up to 40 to 60 minutes a day. It doesn't matter how fast you walk, just walk. The route you take is unimportant, and you don't have to follow the same path every day. If you don't want to walk, try playing tennis, hiking, or biking. If you're young and in good health, then you probably don't need to see a doctor before beginning an exercise program but if you are older or have been inactive for several years, you definitely should consult your physician.

Conditions which indicate a need for medical clearance include:
- High blood pressure
- Heart trouble
- Family history of early stroke or heart attack deaths
- Frequent dizzy spells
- Extreme breathlessness after mild exertion
- Arthritis or other bone problems
- Severe muscular, ligament or tendon problems
- Other known or suspected diseases

A vigorous exercise program involves at least minimal health risks for anyone, so check with your doctor before beginning this type of exercise program.

Taking care of your body is a powerful first step toward mental and emotional health. People who are emotionally healthy are in control of their thoughts, feelings and behaviors. They feel good about themselves and have good relationships. They keep problems in perspective. Emotional health can lead to success in work, relationships, and physical health. In the past it was thought that success makes people happy, but I think it is the other way around. Happy people are more likely to work toward goals, to find the resources they need, and to be successful. Working on emotional health is probably something that many of us neglect even though it probably makes the biggest impact on our daily life. The fact of the matter is that most of us go through life (or are dragged through life) kicking and screaming.

If you've read the previous two sections in this chapter, you may have already begun improving your emotional health. But part of dealing with emotional health is dealing with the past and whatever baggage each of us has. I had acquired a lot of emotional baggage through my life. I had a lot of feelings of frustration, anger, resentment, distrust, and for many of these I didn't know why. For those I did know the source, I had anger toward the individual or situation that caused it. Here is the truth, all of us have had bad or unpleasant life experiences. There is nothing that we can do to take those feelings or experiences away; they will always be part of who we are. However, we can decide what we will do with them in the future.

One of my counselors told me I could never stop those old memories (he called them mental tapes) from running in my mind. What I could do was choose how I responded to them. Having that choice requires creating alternate or optional memories, scenarios, or mental tapes as a preferable option for the negative memory.

Here is an example from my life. During a time when I was learning to work through some of my life issues, I wrote in a journal on a daily basis how I was feeling. During one of my morning journal periods in early December, I found myself typing this at my computer repeatedly, **I hate this, I hate this, I hate this.** I was consumed with these massive feelings of anger which I could not describe nor define. I didn't understand where they were coming from or why they were there. So I began to explore the questions "what makes me mad" and "what is it that I hate." I needed to explore where these feeling were coming from. I began by listing all the things that came to my mind such as routines during the holidays which were not my normal ones (traveling, buying extra food, buying more and more gifts, spending time with relatives, social events, etc.). The list was long but it had one thing in common, it all had to do with the holiday season.

I remembered that the holidays when I was a kid were extremely stressful. They involved alcohol and family fighting and crying myself to sleep. I hated that time of year. Over the years I conditioned myself to even hate the winter months, and especially the long holiday seasons of Thanksgiving, Christmas, and New

Year's. In order to change my behavior I had to recondition my response to those memories. To do that I had to create new memories, so now I often spend my long holiday season doing disaster relief work or teaching in Mexico. It took several years, but I finally now have a more normal negative response to the holidays—they just cost me too much money!

To help improve emotional health, it is important to discover a sense of contentment for your life and what you are doing. Rediscover or discover for the first time a zest for living and the ability to laugh and have fun. Learn to deal with stress in a productive manner and establish healthy responses to adversity. Discover new flexibility for learning new things and adapting to change. Also, learn to balance work and play, rest and activity, and family. These form a strong foundation for healthy emotions and satisfaction in life.

Spiritual Character

JESUS CHRIST GAVE us eight Beatitudes in the Sermon on the Mount, recorded in the Gospels of Matthew and Luke in the New Testament of the Bible. The Beatitudes reveal to us eight qualities which bring God's blessings: meekness and mercy, poorness in spirit and purity of heart, mourning and hunger, peacemaking and persecution. These qualities are the foundations for spiritual character. The term beatitude comes from the Latin adjective **beatus** which means happy, fortunate, or blissful. The Beatitudes present a set of ideas which focus on love and humility rather than force and demand. Spiritual character-building is a continuous process involving further development of goodness within a person. To develop these qualities, you must first learn to keep things in perspective and to discover how to restore your hope.

Keeping Things in Perspective

For individuals who have a disability, it is very important to learn how to keep things in perspective.

Since becoming a Christian, keeping things in perspective has been much easier for me than before. The first critical step in improving my perspective on things was learning to develop confidence in my ability to solve problems. The most complex of all intellectual functions is problem solving. This is a mental process which is part of a larger process which includes identifying and clarifying a problem. Problem solving often requires slicing the problem into manageable parts, and it also requires taking into consideration the true measure of a situation before reacting.

When we do not keep things in perspective, we run the risk of blowing things out of proportion and over-reacting rather than using sound judgment. A well-developed sense of perspective regarding a problem is vital to prevent small problems from overwhelming us. If we lose perspective, we can end up worrying for hours or even longer about things which may never happen.

Likewise, when we feel upset by a situation and the persons involved in it, we should try to place ourselves in their shoes in order to understand their motivations and actions. Seeing issues from a different angle often makes it easier to solve a problem. In addition, we should not let criticism, negative feedback, or critical judgment by others drive us crazy. When we receive negative feedback, it doesn't necessarily mean the feedback is entirely true. Also, negative feedback or criticism doesn't reflect on our overall character, but instead it may help us change behaviors we haven't noticed in ourselves that we will eventually realize should be changed.

Don't get worked up about problems that are insignificant. Think about things that have bothered you recently and be honest in questioning how important they really were. Sometimes problems occur because we assume the worst about situations and people, and our assumptions may be wrong. Try to ignore the problem awhile and give yourself time to realize that the situation may be much less problematic than you first thought it was.

It is also important to avoid judging others' motives, especially when we tend to assume them to be negative. By suspecting the worst, we actually lose something precious within us. Try detaching yourself from a negative perception of that person for a while in order to evaluate your own thoughts and reactions and decide how accurate they are. Often it is good to sleep on it and see how you feel after the surge of emotional energy has faded. A new day may give you a fresh and more optimistic perspective.

Learning to trust yourself takes time and patience, and it also requires understanding that you must live with the consequences of your decisions. It can especially be difficult to trust your own instincts if they have not proved successful in the past. This is particularly true during adolescence and early adult years when you first begin to experience the responsibilities of adulthood. When away from parents, many young people struggle with the process of making decisions, not knowing whom to consult and whom to ignore, both of which may complicate the issue. The question can also be whether it's best to follow the crowd or go the route less traveled.

This lack of confidence in personal reasoning ability may cause anyone to wonder whether they have enough life experiences to make key decisions. Nevertheless, everyone must learn to trust that little voice inside. Isaiah 30:21 (NKJV of the Bible) advises that

"Your ears shall hear a word behind you, saying,
'This is the way, walk in it,'
Whenever you turn to the right hand
Or whenever you turn to the left."

The way to build strength in your ability to hear and trust that little voice is to be quiet and listen. You must take time just being quiet—walking on the beach, taking a shower, running, being by yourself, meditating, or reading your Bible and praying. When you stay busy, busy, busy, going, going, going, it's very hard for that little voice to be heard. Try spending time every day sitting quietly and listening to your inner voice. (I like to spend this quiet time reading scripture and praying.) It will amaze you to see what useful ideas and insights will come to you in this silence.

Strategies for Restoring Hope

One of my earliest counselors advised me to write about my deepest thoughts and feelings, to spend time in meditation, and become involved in spiritual practices. I did and still do all of these, but the one which works best for me is spiritual in nature. My personal strategy for restoring hope is based in my faith. The benefit of being a Christian is that the Holy Spirit who dwells within us convicts us of what is wrong and then inspires us the desire to follow God. When I follow God, people who observe my life should be able to see behaviors which God considers to be right. The analogy Paul used to describe the lives of the believers at Corinth was "... you are an epistle of Christ, ministered to by us, written not with ink but by the Spirit of the living God, not on tablets of stone but on tablets of flesh, that is, of the heart" (2 Corinthians 3:3 New King James version of the Bible).

Every Christian is guaranteed a place in the eternal kingdom of God. Our physical lives on earth are short in comparison with eternal lives which last forever. Believing in Jesus fills our lives with joyful anticipation of the destination that awaits us. Becoming a Christian isn't just an insurance policy for heaven after we die; instead, its benefits begin immediately. And one of those benefits is that God comes alongside of us and helps us not to fall or be destroyed by the circumstances of life. The Bible states that "every spiritual blessing in heavenly places" is available only "in Christ" (Ephesians 1:3). Here is a short list of spiritual blessings found in Christ:

- Forgiveness of sins (Acts 2:38)
- An abundant life with purpose (John 10:10; Ecclesiastes 12:13)
- Divine help in your prayers (Romans 8:26)
- Divine help in resisting temptation (1 Corinthians 13:10)
- Divine protection from evil (2 Thessalonians 3:3)

- Confidence that your physical necessities will be provided (Matthew 6:33; Mark 10:29-30)
- A heavenly inheritance reserved for you (Ephesians 1:11; 1 Peter 1:4)
- An indescribable inner peace (Philippians 4:7)
- Trusting in grace instead of your own ability (Titus 3:5)
- The abiding presence of God with you (Matthew 28:20; Revelation 3:10)
- Abounding love toward others (1 Thessalonians 3:12-13).

There are other spiritual blessings which could be added to this list but these are a good solid start.

Christ will provide each of us fullness and purpose in our lives. No matter how worldly our present life is now, there is still a heavenly purpose if we are willing to walk close to Jesus. Galatians 5:22 tells us that, "the fruit of the Spirit is love, joy, peace, patience, kindness, goodness, faithfulness, gentleness, and self-control." In Philippians 4:7, the Apostle Paul tells us that "the peace of God, which transcends all understanding, will guard your hearts and your minds in Christ Jesus." Each of us can have this inner peace and joy that comes only from knowing Jesus as Lord of our lives. It is this inner peace and joy which gives me the spiritual character and strength to fight through and overcome daily obstacles that otherwise could prevent me from being resilient.

Final Thoughts

KEYS TO MY current success are self-understanding and self-acceptance. In addition to these, I build on my special skills and talents. I set realistic goals and identify supportive adults (family members, friends, and colleagues) to encourage my resolve to find success in life. Werner (1999) found these same components in her research on individuals with disabilities who succeed in spite of their extreme challenges.

According to Rutter (1979), no one is totally secure and everyone has a point in which they fail, and that is what we call normal. Werner (1999) suggests that humans then often attempt to shift the balance point from a weakness to areas of strength. They shift this balance either by decreasing exposure to risk factors and/or stressful events by increasing their number of available protective factors. This ability to shift balance is called resilience. Simply stated, resilience can be defined as the ability to cope successfully in the face of significant adversity or risk. This capability can and often develops and changes over time. My resilience is

grounded in the following eleven "I statements."
I, Richard Evans,
- have strengths and talents, and I need to use them.
- have difficulties and challenges, and I need to define the things which cause me difficulty and make a plan to manage them.
- need to be a goal setter and develop realistic goals. I will start by asking "What's at least one thing I know I can accomplish today to help me move toward achieving one or more of my goals?"
- need to review and work on my goals regularly. Life is constantly in motion and my goals need to be current and relevant.
- need to establish good and useful relationships: I will partner with close family members, friends, and others who care about me and will accept their help and support.
- can see obstacles as potential opportunities. I will stop seeing stressful events as barriers and will recognize them as chances to grow and mature.
- understand that change is a normal part of life. I will accept circumstances which cannot be changed in order to focus on circumstances which can be changed.
- have the right to be proactive and take decisive actions. By taking decisive actions rather than detaching from problems, stressing out, and/or wishing they would go away, I will

manage my problems more effectively.
- can have a positive view of myself. Developing confidence in my ability to solve problems and trusting my instincts will strengthen my resilience.
- have the ability to keep things in perspective. I will not blow an event or problem out of proportion. I will remind myself of this quote credited to Dr. Thomas Walton, President of Texas A&M University in 1939: "The difficult things we handle immediately; the impossible take a little longer." In other words, I can manage anything if I am willing to make the effort.
- have a Higher Power who cares for me and will help me overcome or conquer my challenges.

What Went Wrong

A lot of things went wrong in my life. My numerous at-risk factors began in early childhood and continued throughout my school experiences. My teachers were not prepared to teach children who did not learn in the typical manner. Also, no early intervention programs were available to help develop my basic reading skills in the primary grades. Fortunately for students today, most teachers know more about reading problems and academic difficulties or can find helpful resources.

Consider some of what we know now. According to Gambrell, Morrow, Neuman, and Pressley (1999), literacy practices found in schools today should include direct teaching of decoding and comprehension strategies, reading for authentic meaning, and using a variety of assessment techniques to reach instructional objectives. In addition, Morrow, Tracey, Woo, and Pressley (1999) documented a number of key teacher practices which foster literacy learning. These include extended time to develop reading skills, a balanced approach to instruction (recognizing whole words as well as learning the alphabetic principle), basic instruction on specific needs, and higher teachers' expectations for all students. Research over the past 15 years has suggested that a number of components contribute to improved acquisition of reading skills for most children. These components include instruction in phonemic awareness, the alphabetic principle, fluency in word and text reading, vocabulary instruction, and instruction in reading comprehension strategies (Chard & Dickson, 1999; Duffy-Hester, 1999; National Reading Panel, 2000; Reading Summit, 1998). Fletcher and Lyon (1998) also suggest that instruction should take place within a literature-rich environment which offers a combination of decodable and predictable books to assist readers in the development of adequate reading skills.

In 2000, the National Reading Panel recommended that effective reading instruction consists of three steps. First, children should be taught to break apart and manipulate the sounds in words (phonemic awareness). Then, they should be made aware that these sounds (phonemes) are represented by letters of the alphabet. Finally, they should be taught how to blend these sounds together to form words. This is the fundamental process of alphabetic principle or phonics instruction. They noted that instruction should be functional, useful, and contextual and should be planned, systematic, and explicit to have the most value (Fielding-Barnsley, 1997). I feel sure that I could have benefited from such an inclusive reading program in my early years of school.

Back on Track

In this section, I highlight a number of strategies which are supported by research that I have used to improve my own reading ability. The first focuses on the development of skills in phonemic awareness. According to Pennington, et al. (1990), phonemic awareness (PA) among adults diagnosed with dyslexia was found to be extremely low. Furthermore, adults with dyslexia scored significantly lower than non-dyslexic adults on tasks placed progressively greater demands on phonological processing ability (Shaywitz, et al. 1998). In two additional studies, adults diagnosed with dyslexia were found to continue to have poor phonemic awareness (PA) into adulthood (Bruck, 1992; Scarborough, 1984). Non-disabled good readers' PA improved as they got older and progressed through school, but this was not the case for those with dyslexia (Bruck, 1992). In other studies the level of PA found among older dyslexics was similar to the undeveloped phonemic awareness skills reported in individuals who were illiterate (Scliar-Cabral, Morais, Nepomuceno, & Kolinsky, 1997).

Related to learners with a reading disability such as dyslexia, what is true for non-disabled readers may not be true for beginning adult readers who are reading disabled. Older learners and other non-traditional emergent readers benefit most from phonics instruction that proceeds from whole to part based on analysis and synthesis of meaningful language. Focusing instruction on word families (words that end in the same letters and rhyme—such as the words "can" and "man," for example) can be a staring place young struggling learners. For more examples, see the 37 most common "chunks" and some of the words they make up by Wylie & Durrell (1970).

Word families are also known as "chunks," and they can greatly help students understand the inconsistent English language by providing some predictable patterns within words. As I learned to read, I began to pick up these patterns, but not without effort. Still they helped me learn to decode words. When an older student's attention is directed toward these same patterns, they will be able to unravel the many apparently unrelated sounds of our English language. Once students become familiar with the 37 most familiar chunks, they can use them to decode hundreds of words (Wylie & Durrell, 1970).

Additionally, I worked on understanding what good reading and good readers should be. The best way to communicate what reading is all about is to have someone or some device demonstrate (model) the use of printed materials, and this is especially effective when the modeler explains what he or she is doing and thinking and why (the think-aloud process). As a model for good reading, I used "Books on Tape," family and friends, and "text to speech software." The think aloud strategy is a great way to help students get a good look at how skilled readers construct meaning from text.

When skilled readers approach a text for the first time, they unconsciously summon any and all information or background they have in relation to the topic, idea, people/characters, setting, historical context, author, similar events, etc. This process provides a strong foundation for understanding what they will read; it helps them to make sense of the new text. This is an important step which inexperienced readers often skip over. When teaching reading at the secondary level, teachers should keep in mind what we already know and do implicitly and then make that process clear for our students, especially for struggling readers. Think-Aloud strategies encourage students to talk about the book which then promotes their engagement with the text.

In addition, I used Active Reading tools to interact with what was being read. I learned that when reading a document in detail, it often helps my comprehension to highlight, underline, and add footnotes as I read. This reinforces the information as I read and helps me to review important points later. Doing this also helps me keep my mind focused on the material and stops it from wandering. This was obviously something that I could not do with materials that I didn't own, but I found that by photocopying the document, I could then read and make my notes on the photocopies. I used an assortment of different color highlighters to identify main points, supporting details, and terms; color taps right into visual memory. I used flagging (tabs on the pages) to identifying important textual locations so they could be found quickly when needed. I used marginal notes to make comments or jot down questions relevant to local paragraphs to provide visual cues when I went back over the text for a review of the materials. I also spent time writing section summaries to condense information to ensure that I understood, could remember, and could apply in writing the information that I had read. Lastly, I tried to identify the progression of main points in the material in order to commit the information to memory and provide a reference for future use. This was also very useful when I needed to write about a specific topic or text.

Reading comprehension and vocabulary knowledge are closely related, and numerous studies have shown the strong correlation between the two (see Nagy, 1988; Smith, 1997). Knowledge of word meanings (vocabulary) is critical to reading comprehension (Marzano, Pickering, & Pollock, 2001). Levy and Lysynchuk (1997) reported that rapid acquisition of new reading vocabulary came faster through instruction of word segmentation (prefixes, root words, and suffixes) than with whole-word instruction. Jenkins, Stein, and Wysocki (1984) found that when learning a new word in context (without instruction), students need to be exposed to the word at least six times before they have enough experience with it to understand and remember its meaning. When studying vocabulary, Stahl and Fairbanks (1986) found that direct teaching of general vocabulary affected learning positively, and that direct instruction of words which were critical for understanding new information produced the most powerful learning.

As a final point, I started improving my own vocabulary knowledge by first listening to my wife or a computer read aloud text passages that I needed to learn. This listening comprehension activity was followed by my retelling what was in the text using vocabulary words I was learning. My notes and copies of written text were also used for improving reading fluency as well as serving as a multi-sensory word recognition activity—I not only saw a word as I read it but also felt and heard myself speak it aloud. It should be emphasized that my initial improvement in decoding words also helped improve my vocabulary and reading comprehension. In addition to the strategies I described, I also had one-to-one instruction for a year by a trained tutor in the city's Adult Literacy program

Technology was also a crucial tool that facilitated my academic success. Assistive technologies such as text readers and "speech to text writers" help students by compensating for functional limitations in order to enhance and increase their learning, independence, communication, and choices. These technologies allowed me to have access to high interest reading materials, adapt them to my personal reading level, and to write without focusing on spelling problems until I was ready to edit. They also provided tools for looking up definitions, pronunciation, and grammar as well as providing access to a thesaurus. All of these were made available with one technology aid, my computer.

When teaching students who have not learned to read well in elementary school, both general and special education teachers are often challenged by how to provide reading instruction that meets their needs at the middle and high school levels. My recommendation is to focus on the effective reading steps recommended by the National Reading Panel (2000). Start with instruction in phonemic awareness, followed by phonics instruction by using grade level materials. Use research practices which foster literacy learning using a balanced or comprehensive approach, carefully designing delivery of instruction in phonemic awareness, phonics (alphabetic principle), fluency in word and text reading. Include instruction in vocabulary and reading comprehension strategies. Effective instruction is fundamental and functional, useful and contextual. It should also be planned, systematic, and explicit to the student.

Finally, use your own creative methods and listen to your inner voice as you think about a particular student. Methods I devised which helped me personally may also help your struggling students. If your district has a volunteer program, please welcome individuals into your classroom to work with below-level readers one-to-one when possible. Peer tutoring has also been used successfully to help struggling readers. If your district does not yet have assistive technologies, please explain their benefits to a school administrator.

After submitting a request several times which lists the advantages of its use by students with learning difficulties, your request may eventually be approved.

If at all possible, do not ignore the needs of any struggling reader. All students can learn. Finding ways to help them learn will be some of your most rewarding experiences as a teacher—ones you will treasure for a lifetime.

Reference

Ballard, J., Ramirez, B., & Zantal-Wiener, K. (1987). Public Law 94-142, Section 504, and Public Law 99-457: Understanding what they are and are not. Reston, VA: The Council for Exceptional Children.

Bear, D. R., Templeton, S., Invernizzi, M. & Johnston, F. (1996). Words their way: Word study for phonics, vocabulary and spelling instruction. Englewood Cliffs, NJ: Merrill.

Blevins, W. (1998). Phonics from A to Z. New York, NY: Scholastic Professional Books.

Bruck, M. (1992). Persistence of dyslexics' phonological deficits. *Developmental Psychology*, 28(5), 874-886.

Chard, D., & Dickson, S. (1999). Phonological awareness: Instructional and assessment guidelines. *Intervention in School and Clinic,* 34 (5), 261-270.

Duffy-Hester, A. (1999). Teaching struggling readers in elementary school classrooms: A review of classroom reading programs and principles for instruction. *The Reading Teacher*, 52 (5)480-495.

Fletcher, J. M., & Lyon, G. R. (1998). Reading: A research-based approach. In W. M. Evans (Ed.), What's gone wrong in America's classrooms (pp. 49-90). Stanford, CA: Hoover Institution Press.

Gambrell, L., Morrow, L., Neuman, S., & Pressley, M. (1999). Best practices in literacy instruction. New York: Guilford.

Heward, W. (2003). Exceptional Children (7th ed): An Introduction to Special Education. Upper Saddle River, New Jersey: Columbus, OH.

Masten, A. S. (1994). Resilience in individual development: Successful adaptation despite risk and adversity. In M. C. Wang & E. W. Gordon (Eds.), Educational resilience in inner-city America (pp. 3-25). Hillsdale, MJ: Erlbaum.

Miller, M. & Fritz, M. F. (1998). A demonstration of resilience. Intervention in school and clinic, 33

Mattis, S. (1978)."Dyslexia Syndromes: A Working Hypothesis." In DYSLEXIA. New York: Oxford University Press.

Morrow, L., Tracey, D., Woo, D., & Pressley, M. (1999). Characteristics of exemplary first-grade literacy instruction. *The Reading Teacher*, 52(5), 462-476.

Moustafa, M. (1997). Beyond traditional phonics: Research discoveries and reading instruction. Portsmouth, NH: Heinemann.

National Reading Panel. (2000). National Reading

Panel releases report on research-based approaches to reading instruction; Expert panel offers its groundbreaking findings to U.S. Congress and the nation. Washington, D.C. Retrieved November 10, 2002, from http://www.nationalreadingpanel.org/Press/press_releases.htm.

Reading Summit (1998). Remarks as prepared for delivery by U.S. Secretary of Education Richard W. Riley. Washington, DC. Retrieved November 10, 2002, from http://www.ed.gov/inits/readingsummit/readsum.html.

Roos, P. (1970). Trends and issues in special education for the mentally retarded. *Education and Training of the Mentally Retarded,* 5, 51-61.

Slavin, R. E. (1989). Here to stay--or gone tomorrow?. *Educational Leadership.* 47 p. 3.

Smith. D. (2004). Introduction to special education: Teaching in an age of opportunity. Allyn & Bacon. Boston, 5th ed.

Swanson, C. B. (2004). Graduation rates: real kids, real numbers. *Principal Leadership* (Middle School Ed.) 5(4) p. 22-7.

Rutter, M. (1979). Protective factors in children's responses to stress and disadvantage. In Primary Prevention of Psychopathology, Vol. 3: Social Competence in Children, ed. by M.W. Kent and J.ER. olf. Hanover, NH: University Press of New England, 49-74.

Rutter, M. (2001). Psychosocial adversity: Risk, resilience and recovery. In J. M. Richman & M. W. Fraser

(Eds.), The context of youth violence: Resilience, risk, and protection (pp. 13-41). Westport, CT: Praeger Publishers (5), 265-271.

Sameroff, A. J., Seifer, R. Baldwin, A., & Baldwin, C. (1993). Stability of intelligence from preschool to adolescence: The influence of social and family risk factors. *Child Development*, 64, 80-97.

Shaywitz, S., Shaywitz, B. A., Pugh, K. R., Fulbright, R. K., Constable, R. T., Mencl, W. E., Shankweiler, D. P., Liberman, A. M., Skudlarski, P., Fletcher, J. M., Katz, L., Marchione, K. E., Lacadie, C., Gatenby, C., & Gore, J. C. (1998). Functional disruption in the organization of the brain for reading in dyslexia. Proceedings of the National Academy of Sciences USA, 95, 2636-2641.

Pennington, B., Orden, G. C. V., Smith, S., Green, P. A., & Haith, M. M. (1990). Phonological processing skills and deficits in adult dyslexics. *Child Development*, 61(6), 1753-1778.

Scarborough, H. S. (1984). Continuity between childhood dyslexia and adult reading. British Journal of Psychology, 75, 329-348.

Scliar-Cabral, L., Morais, J., Nepomuceno, L., & Kolinsky, R. (1997). The awareness of phonemes: So close - so far away. *International Journal of Psycholinguistics*, 13(38), 211-240.

Werner, E. (1990). Protective factors and individual resilience. In Handbook of Early Childhood Intervention, ed. by Samuel Meisels and Jack Shonkoff. New York:Cambridge University.

Werner, E. E. (1999). Risk and protective factors in the lives of children with high-incidence disabilities. In R. Gallimore, L. P. Bernheimer, D. L. MacMillan,

Wylie, R.E., & Durrell, D.D. (1970). Teaching vowels through phonograms. *Elementary English,* 47, 787-791. Portsmouth, NH: Heinemann.

Young, B.A. (2002). Public high school dropouts and completers from common core of data: School years 1998-99 to 1999-2000. NCES Report 2002-328. Washington, D.C: U.S. Department of Education, OERI, NCES.

CPSIA information can be obtained at www.ICGtesting.com
Printed in the USA
BVOW061157020512

289239BV00001B/13/P

9 781432 779245